The Death of Modern Management

The Death of Modern Management

How to Lead in the New World Disorder

Jo Owen

A John Wiley & Sons, Ltd., Publication

This edition first published 2009
© 2009 Jo Owen

Registered office

John Wiley & Sons Ltd, The Atrium, Southern Gate, Chichester, West Sussex, PO19
8SQ, United Kingdom

For details of our global editorial offices, for customer services and for information
about how to apply for permission to reuse the copyright material in this book please
see our website at www.wiley.com.

Library of Congress Cataloging-in-Publication Data

Owen, Jo.
    The death of modern management : how to lead in the new world disorder / Jo Owen.
        p. cm.
    Includes bibliographical references and index.
    ISBN 978-0-470-68285-2
    1. Management.   2. Leadership.   I. Title.
    HD31.0844 2009
    658.4′092–dc22

                                                                            2009040196

A catalogue record for this book is available from the British Library.

Set in 10.5/15pt Monotype Janson by Toppan Best-set Premedia Limited
Printed in Great Britain by TJ International Ltd, Padstow, Cornwall, UK

Contents

Acknowledgements

A central theme of this book is that we are all small islands of expertise in a vast ocean of knowledge. However much we may know about our own area, we depend hugely on the talent of other people to make things happen. This is especially true of authors. If we make any sense, which some will dispute, it is because we are able to call on a huge hinterland of people and experience who contribute their knowledge and talent.

This book is based on 30 years of working with nearly 100 of the best, and a few of the worst, organisations on our planet: from Japan, across Asia to Saudi Arabia, through Europe and to North America, I have been very fortunate to work with inspiring and insightful leaders who have helped shape the views in this book. It is impossible to assign any order to their contributions, so I will list them in the order in which I have worked with them.

Tony Johnson is largely to blame for me writing any books at all: he inspired me to first put pen to paper. Over decades, James Kelly has been an extraordinary mentor and supporter, whose contribution I will never be able to repay fully. Although this book is not kind to academics, there have been some exceptional professors who have been very kind to me. Philip Kotler went out of his way to help me with my career and my writing. He is a role model for the constant renewal of intellectual capital. Nigel Nicholson always brings me back to earth when I get too big for my boots, adding insight and humour as he does so.

My not-for-profit work has opened my eyes to different ways of working. Sally Morgan and Heath Monk of Future Leaders; Sharath Jeevan of Teaching Leaders; Brett Wigdortz and Julia Cleverdon of Teach First; and Juliet Hope and Mari Simpson of Start Up all show what can be achieved with a great deal of passion and remarkably little resource. They are the antidote to resource rich corporate thinking.

More recently, I have had the pleasure of working with some wonderful colleagues who have continued to help me with my learning journey: Laura Watkins and Shani Ospina of Cognitas are outstanding; Stephen Mansbridge of AGM has been more than generous with his time, support and patience. Mary Powell and Nithi Anandan have, in their respective ways, saved what is left of my sanity on many occasions.

Inevitably, a book like this is not possible without a publisher who shows belief and confidence in new ideas: I am hugely grateful to Wiley for their commitment and in particular to Tom Clark and Ellen Hallsworth for backing the book and to Ellen for some very diligent and effective editing. Also at Wiley, Nick Mannion, Julia Bezzant and Louise Cheer have led a whole firm effort in bringing this book to market. Finally, I am always indebted to my family for supporting me and tolerating my mutterings and ramblings as I have pursued my various ideas, so my thanks to Hiromi, Gaie, Toby and Jane.

As ever, wherever there are faults, they are all mine.

Introduction

How We Got Here and Where We Are Going

Modern management is dying under the weight of its own contradictions.

This book does not predict a revolution. It maps the revolution that is happening before our eyes. The old world of simplistic formulas for strategy, finance and leadership no longer works. The credit crunch exposed fatal weaknesses in finance. It also exposed a deeper crisis which has been brewing for longer: a crisis of management. The easy certainties of the past are over. Producer power is being challenged by consumers; shareholders are losing out to managers and the West is losing ground to Asia. As with all revolutions, this revolution is about power. The old order is giving way to a new world disorder. For some, this represents great risk; for others, it represents great opportunity.

Modern management promised progress through science, efficiency and insight. Since the Industrial Revolution, this has led to huge progress and prosperity. But modern management is now reaching its end game. There is no more advantage to be gained from doing the same as everyone else. We may run hard to improve our operations, but if everyone else is improving at the same rate we find we have run hard to stay still relative to the competition. If we all do the same analysis and enter the same markets, we are collectively doomed to fail. The universal truths which modern management sought have led to self-defeating conformity.

We are now embarking on the third wave of management. The first, pre-modern, wave of management was barely capable of making progress. Management, to the extent it existed, was the product of tradition carefully handed down from master to apprentice and jealously protected by the closed shop of craft guilds. The Renaissance and then the Enlightenment paved the way for the Industrial Revolution by freeing minds to question, measure, analyse and improve. This was the revolution which led to the second wave of management: modern management.

The third wave of management is quietly burying the certainties and assumptions that have been inherited from the previous waves of management. Organisations are moving from command and control to cooperation and commitment; we are struggling to manage the change from deficit to surplus of information, knowledge and communication; customers are fragmenting and globalising at the same time; firms are hollowing out and reconfiguring themselves; accounting and capital is floundering as value shifts from tangibles to intangibles.

The new world disorder is with us now. Changing technology is a small part of it: changing the way we think is the big part of it. Some businesses and managers intuitively understand what it takes to succeed in an increasingly uncertain world. Others do not understand and simply see the change as risk. This book will help you chart your way through the revolution, turning risk into opportunity and challenges into success.

Six snapshots and a movie of the revolution

From the Boston Tea Party to the storming of the Bastille and the uprising on the battleship Potemkin, every revolution has its symbolic moments. Management revolutions are slower and less bloodthirsty than political revolutions, but they also have their symbolic and defining moments.

Through the fog of history we can see at least six moments in management which define its past and shape its future. Three of the moments define the ascent of modern management. Three of the moments symbolise its decline.

Snapshot One: an apple falls on Isaac Newton's head
Isaac Newton is not normally seen as the godfather of modern management, but he is. Legend has it that an apple falling on his head led him to enquire why apples always fell downwards, not upwards. The consequences of his enquiries shaped the world of science and the world of management. In 1687 he published *Principia*. Once Newton had discovered the laws of classical physics, he opened up the floodgates of the Enlightenment. For sure, the seeds of the Enlightenment had been sown by Copernicus, Galileo and others who challenged the orthodoxy of the Church, but it was with Newton that the Enlightenment finally bloomed into an unstoppable force. Following Newton, scientific enquiry became the spearhead of progress, not just in science but also in agriculture,

industry and management. Everyone wanted to discover the universal rules which would help us understand and improve the world around us.

Modern management has helped transform the world since Newton's time. Newton was born in 1643 in the early stages of another revolution: a civil war which led to the execution of King Charles I. King Charles lived without iPods, i, MTV, electricity, running water, cars, planes, dental care, fridges, freezers or central heating. Modern management has helped turn unimaginable luxuries into everyday necessities. To understand how this came about, we need to step forwards another 100 years or so to the dawn of the Industrial Revolution.

Snapshot Two: Adam Smith observes the pin makers of Gloucester

1776 was a revolutionary year. America declared Independence and, just as revolutionary, Adam Smith published *Wealth of Nations*. What Isaac Newton did for physics, Adam Smith attempted to do for economics. He succeeded where no alchemist had ever succeeded before: he discovered laws which created wealth out of nothing. His most famous breakthrough was to observe pin making in Gloucester. One skilled pin maker would struggle to make 20 pins a day if he did every task himself. Ten semi-skilled workers, each focused on one small part of the task, could produce "upwards of 48,000 pins in a day". Adam Smith had observed division of labour, volume production, de-skilling and specialisation. This was not just an economic revolution, it was a management revolution. The resulting Industrial Revolution swept away the old craft guilds and swept in unprecedented poverty, prosperity and progress.

Adam Smith helped introduce the Enlightenment disciplines of observation, measurement, analysis and improvement into the world of commerce and management. Once started, the treadmill of progress appeared to be unstoppable.

Snapshot Three: The first Ford Model T rolls off the production line, 1908

From Adam Smith to Henry Ford is a small intellectual step and a huge economic leap. Ford's revolutionary moving production line changed the economics of car making. Out went all the hand built cars made by skilled craftsmen: in came semi-skilled, highly specialised workers producing a standard product at low cost. Ford took cost reduction to the limit, integrating the business all the way from owning forests for the wood he needed, through to offering customers any colour, as long as it was black.

If Henry Ford represented the practice of modern management, Frederick Taylor represented the theory. In 1911 he laid out *Scientific Management*. In the tradition of Newton and the Enlightenment, Taylor used observation and measurement to understand how productivity can be maximised. He developed time and motion studies, saw that work breaks raised productivity rather than interrupted it, and recommended that different sorts of people should do different sorts of job. These are commonplace ideas which were so revolutionary in their day that Taylor was dismissed from his first employer, Bethlehem Steel.

At this point, the science of modern management went into overdrive. GM, under Alfred Sloan, upstaged Ford with effective market segmentation. Sloan responded to Ford's idea of a single type of car "for the great multitude" with "a car for every purse and purpose": market segmentation had arrived on an industrial scale with Chevrolet, Oldsmobile, Buick and Cadillac all carefully organised into different business units targeted at different customer age and wealth groups. By the time Sloan published *My Years at General Motors* in 1963 it appeared that the apotheosis of modern management had been reached.

By now, the West seemed to be on an inevitable, unstoppable ladder to prosperity. It would only be a matter of time before we would all be commuting on personal aircraft and possibly on personal spacecraft to our holidays on the moon. Something, somewhere, went wrong.

Snapshot Four: Akio Morita hears the
ghetto blasters

The young Akio Morita, founder of Sony, was in New York and observed gangs of teenagers with boom boxes on their shoulders. Most people saw nuisance, heard pollution and felt fear when the gangs appeared. Akio Morita saw opportunity. He saw that young people wanted to be with music all the time. He made their dreams come true with the Sony Walkman, the first truly personal music system. The Walkman leads in a straight line to iPods and all the other basic necessities of modern teenage life.

Akio Morita is one of several possible standard bearers for the assault on modern management as the West perceived it. He is joined by Soichira Honda who saw that not all bikers were Hell's Angels on Harley-Davidsons: he produced smaller motorbikes for families, fishing and fun. The motorbike was the first step to global success in engines and autos. Just as Honda and Toyota assaulted the auto market, so Canon assaulted the copier market by turning it on its head. Canon did not follow Xerox with big, expensive centralised copiers which had to be leased. Instead they produced small, cheap, slow copiers which could be at the side of every executive.

The Japanese revolution blew away vast swathes of Western industry: consumer electronics, auto manufacturing and computers. This was not meant to happen. Giants like Ford, GM, Westinghouse, Philips, Wang and DEC should not have been threatened by tiny upstarts from the East. To make matters worse, they were not just competing on the basis of cheap labour. Anyone who has eaten in a Tokyo restaurant recently will wonder if they are buying a meal or buying the restaurant when the bill is ever so politely presented to them. Japan has not been cheap for the last 20 years. These upstarts were using the very methods of modern management that the West had discovered: moving production lines, market segmentation and quality systems devised by an American: Edward Deming.

China is now following in the footsteps of Japan, but with eight times the population. In 2004 an unheard of Chinese company, Lenovo, bought the PC business of IBM, which had been the godfather of the modern PC industry. The world has tilted on its axis from west to east. Already China and Japan own $1.5 trillion of US government debt, or about $5000 for every US citizen. The US had a trade deficit with China and Japan of $338 billion in 2008 (over $1000 for every US citizen). These imbalances show that the days of American hegemony are under threat: other countries and other ways of doing business are challenging the old order.

In the right hands (Western, if you are Western), modern management was the road to riches. In the wrong hands, it seemed to be the highway to hell. The first cracks in modern management were starting to appear. The universal rules of strategy and success suddenly seemed either not to apply, or to be a very double edged sword. Uncertainty began to intrude into a world which had been very certain and self-assured to the point of complacency.

Snapshot Five: the dot.com bust
In 2000, the dot com boom turned to bust. All the brave talk of a new paradigm turned to dust. The only winners from that bust were the senior executives of the top 20 corporate busts who took out a cool $2.6 billion in compensation for  bankrupting their start ups and losing all their shareholders' money: it was a play which was going to enjoy a big revival when the credit crunch came along. In the credit crunch, senior bankers took the place of dot.com executives in cashing in at the expense of the shareholders they ruined.

Both the dot.com bust and the credit crunch raise the same question: who has the power? Marx firmly believed that power lay with owners of capital who would so fully exploit the workers, that the workers would eventually rise up in revolt and usher in a Communist paradise (complete with labour camps, bread queues, pogroms and secret police on every doorstep). Writing in 1867, Marx might have been right about where the power lay. But power has shifted. Power no longer resides with the owners of capital: it resides with the controllers of capital, with the top managers and key executives of public companies. The dot.com bust and credit crunch have shown that managers have become very good at maximising their rewards while offloading all the risk onto the shareholders: that is an arrangement which would have been unthinkable both to Marx, and to his archetypal enemy, the evil mill owner.

The workers' revolution did not come about through violence. It came about through education and skills. No longer could workers be coerced: command and control management started to give way. Employers found that employees had options. The days of the one-company towns, such as McDonald, Ohio (Carnegie Steel), Port Sunlight (Unilever) or Bourneville (Cadbury) were over. Employees had choices about where to work and welfare if they could not or would not work. Managers lost power: they had to discover the subtle arts of motivation and building commitment, a far remove from the time and motion studies of Frederick Taylor.

The dot.com bust and credit crunch showed that the organisational certainties of modern management could no longer be taken for granted. The key assets of the business were no longer the plant and the equipment but the people. Unlike machinery, employees can walk away if they do not like the company. Managers were learning to manage in fundamentally different ways from before. Managing people is far harder than managing machines.

Snapshot Six: Ford and GM go begging to Congress, 2008

In December 2008, the Chief Executives of the Big Three auto manufacturers went to Washington to plead for bail out money. It was a humbling experience. They had been forced to ditch their fancy private jets and had to drive to Washington. If Ford and GM had been at the vanguard of modern management, they now found themselves in the vanguard of its demise. Over decades, talented management had streamlined processes, improved quality, reduced costs, reorganised, innovated and introduced new models. They had done everything modern managers were meant to do. And yet their CEOs had been reduced to corporate beggars looking to survive on government welfare. For Rick Wagoner, the CEO of GM, this was particularly galling: Alfred Sloan had been the pin-up boy of modern management and GM. In March 2009 Wagoner was ousted: he had turned into the fall guy for GM, and possibly for the failures of modern management.

The auto manufacturers were not alone in their misery. The banks were in an even worse state. Investment banks disappeared as a species within a few months: Lehman Brothers went bust, Bears Sterns and Merrill Lynch got taken over and Goldman Sachs and Morgan Stanley quickly made themselves into commercial banks. The bill to the taxpayer for the bailout is $700 billion and rising.

When one company runs into trouble it reflects one company's mistakes. When two entire industries go under something bigger is going on. Part of the "something bigger" is recession, which exposes all the malpractice and mistakes of boom time. But that is not the whole story. There is another theme which links the dot. com bust, the problems of the auto makers and the demise of the investment banks.

In each case smart managers were all doing smart analysis and coming up with smart solutions. But the solutions which were smart individually were suicidal collectively. They had not discovered the alchemist's formula for turning base metal into gold. They had found the opposite, the formula for destroying vast amounts of shareholder wealth. This was the Enlightenment dream turned nightmare: universal laws which promised so much, delivered the opposite of what they promised. Universal laws seemed to turn prosperity into poverty.

The credit crunch not only exposed malpractices of the previous boom. It exposed some of the fundamental flaws of modern management. When every company does the same rational analysis and arrives at the same rational solution, you do not discover competitive advantage: you discover competitive suicide. In science it helps when the same different people apply the same rules and arrive at the same solution: it confirms the validity of the scientific theory. The knowledge economy is based on innovation, diversity and myriad small failures. Simplistic formulas for strategy, finance and leadership encourage conformity, not innovation. Communist conformity helped bring about economic collapse in Eastern Europe: corporatist conformity brought about economic chaos in the West. When managers all arrive at the same solution and do the same thing, in financial markets or elsewhere, disaster ensues. Competitive advantage does not come from being the same as everyone else: it comes from being different in a relevant way.

During boom times, it does not matter that everyone is doing the same thing. If demand is strong, then all the competitors can make money. When the tide is in all ships float. When boom turns to bust and the tide of demand turns, many ships will find themselves stranded. Formulas for success become formulas for failure.

If the credit crunch illustrates the danger of formulaic strategies, that is good news for management. Managers should not be slaves to a theory: they need to create their own future, decide their own rules and control their own destiny. This world of disorder is liberating and unnerving in equal measure.

From snapshots to a movie

When a revolution happens over 300 years, it is hard to see the changes from day to day. Like Charles Darwin, we need a long perspective. Darwin trained as a geologist. Thinking in geological time, which allows for continents drifting and the sea bed to rise into mountains, gave him the time perspective to see that animals could evolve and change dramatically over millions of generations. In geological time, a 300-year revolution happens faster than the geological eye can blink.

In that spirit, we will now paste our snapshots from the past together to create a movie: we need to pick out the direction and movement of change, rather than focus on isolated moments in history.

The first three snapshots show the relentless rise of modern management. From Newton through Adam Smith, Henry Ford, Alfred Sloan and Frederick Taylor there had been a relentless pursuit of the formula for success: formulas for strategic success, competitive success, operational excellence, managerial success and the formula for managing people.

The last three snapshots show how the orthodoxy of modern management has been fatally undermined, both for strategy and for organisation. The result is liberation for management. Instead of being slaves to a formula, the challenge for management is to create their own rules and their own destiny. To some, this freedom is terrifying: it eliminates the old certainties. For the brave, the new world is one of opportunity.

The movie: In search of magic

The search for magic success formulas in modern management has a long history. To this day, there are academics and consultants churning out their latest theory on how to achieve success: BCG grids, Porter's Five Forces, Hamel and Prahalad on Strategic Intent and Core Competences, Prahalad's protégé Chan Kim on Value

Curves. The hunt for universal strategy formulas is a legacy of the Enlightenment quest for the universal laws of everything. There are two main problems with all these strategy theories:

Apples falling upwards

All the theories are based on cases where the theory has been ret-rofitted onto reality: none of the success stories used to illustrate the theory actually applied the theory that was being touted. Second, each theory is highly selective: they ignore all the exceptions which disprove their theory. If Newton had found even one apple falling upwards, he would have had to change his ideas. Most strategy formulas being touted in the marketplace are full of the strategic equivalent of whole orchards of apples falling upwards. Quite simply, the theories are lousy science which would embarrass any science undergraduate, let alone a professor.

A thousand lemmings can't be wrong …

Universal strategic formulas are, by definition, self-defeating. When everyone does the same analysis and does the same thing, the result is collective suicide. This is the origin of the dot.com bust, the credit crunch and other industry disasters such as the 3G telco auctions and the rush into market making for UK government bonds after liberalisation in 1986. In each case, there was room for a few players to make money. When everyone did the same analysis and chased the same market all the players were acquiring licences to lose money. The problem arises when strategic formulas become a substitute for thinking, instead of an aid for thinking. Then the frameworks become a prison from which there is no escape.

As with strategy, so with organisation. The search for universal rules of success have turned out to be a mirage. All the paradigms of organisational excellence have turned to dust. GM may have represented the summit of best management practice under Alfred Sloan: few managers would care to copy GM nowadays.

One of the most famous attempts to codify and bottle organisational success came 30 years ago. Two McKinsey consultants, Peters and Waterman, decided to decode the formula of successful management by looking at the best companies of the time. They carefully selected those companies which showed sustained and sustainable marketplace success and shareholder value creation. The result was published as *In Search of Excellence*. For a moment, compare these two lists of companies:

A list	B list
DEC	American Express
Wang	Southwest Airlines
Data General	FedEx
Amoco	Coca Cola
Dana	General Electric

There is a myopia about both these lists: they both assume that the only successful organisations which are worth studying or copying must be American. This is a myopia which has been sustained by books such as *Good to Great* which demonstrates an inability to look seriously beyond America. All 11 "Great" companies carefully selected by Jim Collins were American. Since the book was published in 2001, his great companies have suffered: Circuit City has gone bankrupt; Gillette has been taken over; Nucor is struggling to break even and Fannie Mae has been bailed out by government at huge expense. Once again, we find that success is ephemeral: the elixir of corporate youth does not exist. And if we want to find models of success, we need to look beyond America. US markets are being taken over by Japanese and Chinese companies with many more jobs being outsourced to India. No company and no nation has a monopoly on excellence or success.

The A list companies are the ones which *In Search of Excellence* held up as paradigms of excellence. The B list companies, although in existence at the time, were ignored. The problem was not faulty analysis, because the McKinsey analysis was very thorough. The problem is that excellence is ephemeral. What works today may not work tomorrow. What works in America may not work in China. What works in banking may not apply in auto manufacturing. What worked for American companies in the 1970s may not apply to global companies today, because the world has changed. Technology and the internet, globalisation and the rise of Asia are just a few of the changes that means yesterday's formulas do not apply today.

To understand just how ephemeral success is, look back 25 years. In 1984, the FTSE 100 was created: it consisted of the top 100 public companies in the UK. These were the invincible titans of British industry. 25 years later, just 33 of them have survived in the FTSE 100. All the others have been demoted. In the United States, there is a similar story. Only 40 of the Fortune 100 from 25 years ago are still in the Fortune 100. Well over half of all the top companies have been overtaken or taken over inside a generation. Looking slightly further back, just 87 of the original S&P 500 companies from 1957 still exist: less than 20% have survived near the top for 50 years. That is a survival rate which confirms the ephemeral nature of success. We can be sure that many of the paradigms of success which are being celebrated today will be quietly forgotten tomorrow.

Searching for excellence has become as futile as searching for smoke signals in the fog. Excellence, if it exists, is defined only by what works for one company at one time. Excellence is not universal: it is about what fits and what works at any one time. Excellence therefore changes from time to time and from company to company.

At first glance, we appear to be watching a disaster movie: great companies collapse and our roadmaps to the future lead us not to excellence and success, but to ever greater perils. So now let us turn disaster into triumph and see how the death of modern management is a cause for celebration, not for mourning.

For each company that stumbles, there is another eager to take its place. If we focus on the stumbling companies, we are in the disaster movie. If we focus on the companies that are taking their place, we are in the triumph movie. As you look at the list of incumbents and challengers below, there are a few points to hold in mind:

- Many of the challengers were not even on the competitive radar screens of the incumbents 20–30 years ago.
- The challengers lacked all the resources, skills, market power and financial muscle of the incumbents, and yet they have still succeeded.
- Success is not just about new technology: it is about management as well.
- Many more success stories have succeeded by occupying new and uncontested territory: FedEx, Google, Microsoft and MTV have all dominated new or nearly new competitive space.

Incumbents	Challengers
GM, Ford	Toyota, Honda
BA, AA	Southwest Airlines, Ryanair
NBC, BBC	CNN, Sky
ATT, BT	Verizon, Vodafone
Barnes and Noble	Amazon
Xerox	Canon

By turning our attention from the setbacks to the successes, we can see that the end of formulaic modern management is not a problem: it is an opportunity which opens up a whole new world of management. No one knows where this revolution will finish: we are clearly still in the middle of it. We do not know how, or even if, this movie will end. The purpose of this book is to map the revolution to date, and to suggest how managers and organisations can adapt and thrive in the new world of uncertainty and opportunity.

The fog of the future

Through the fog of uncertainty we can see five major strands of the revolution emerging:

Strategic revolution and the challenge of the new world disorder

The collapse of success formulas is the result of the rise of asymmetric competition where challengers do not play to the rules of incumbents. Challengers are playing to their own rules: they create their own market space; they open up new market segments and new ways of looking at the market; they offer new ways of selling through new channels. Technology helps and supports such innovation, but when technology leads innovation the dot.com bust is the result. The strategic revolution is about markets and management, not just technology.

The shift of power

We are witnessing four fundamental shifts in power:

- From shareholders to managers
- From the West to the rest of the world
- From producers to consumers
- From the unskilled to the skilled

Marx would be spinning in his grave: workers are not rebelling against the evil mill owner. Now the media breathlessly report when shareholder dare to "revolt" against managers and vote against them at an AGM. Risk and rewards have moved hugely in favour of skills versus capital: owners take the risk, managers take the reward. Just as managers have more power at work, they have more power and more choice as consumers: power is shifting from producers to consumers. The seismic shift of power from the West is well documented, and is only just starting. These power shifts have far to go and are changing the landscape of business for good.

Knowledge and the disintegration of the firm

Ideas and knowledge, like skills and management, are becoming more important relative to capital. A good idea beats the dull weight of money every time: the great entrepreneurs of today, from Branson to Gates, started with nothing. The importance of knowledge is forcing firms to focus even more on what they are good at. Firms are shifting from high integration to disintegration as they specialise along the value chain. Apple may control production of the iPod, but of the 19 000 people who produce iPods in Asia, only 30 are employed by Apple. The rest work for contractors in Korea, the Philippines, China, Korea and Japan. Increased specialisation across a global value chain creates huge challenges of coordination and integration within and beyond the boundaries of the firm.

Organisations and the collapse of structure

Traditional organisation structures are collapsing, both internally and externally. Internally, command and control functional organisations are giving way to matrix organisations. These are more flexible, but more challenging. For managers, it is easy to hide but hard to shine in a matrix, which requires learning new political and interpersonal skills to make things happen. Externally, the boundaries of organisations are blurring. From the one-company town, which was like a self-sustaining medieval walled city, we have arrived at organisations where many of the critical functions are outsourced.

The world of work: freedom and slavery

Employees are no longer like indentured workers at the mercy of an all-powerful employer. Through skills, affluence, welfare and choice employees have found freedom. With freedom comes responsibility. Employees can no longer count on jobs for life or a paternalistic employer to look after their welfare.

Employees and managers have to look after themselves. This uncertainty creates a new slavery, where managers are tied to the technological shackles of email and are expected to be on call 24/7. Having achieved freedom and power, we need to learn how to use it.

In the following chapters we will explore each of these themes. We will show how the change has come about, what it means to managers and how managers can make the most of each change. The depth and breadth of these changes are huge. To understand the scale of the revolution, consider the abbreviated summary below.

Modern management and the new world disorder compared	Modern management	New world disorder
1. *Strategic revolution*		
Strategy	Analysis, certainty	Experiment, uncertainty
	Competitive warfare	Asymmetric warfare
	Follow prescriptive rules	Change the rules
Marketing	Sell tangible benefits	Sell intangible values
	Make and sell	Co-create
	Single channel	Competing channels
Customers	National class segments	Global lifestyle segment
	Attitudes	Behaviour
	Monolithic, static segments	Mass markets of one

(*Continued*)

Modern management and the new world disorder compared	Modern management	New world disorder
2. Money, information and the shift of power		
Accounting	Departments	Activities
	Standard reporting	Custom reporting
	Tangible assets	Intangible assets
Information	Deficit	Surplus
	Producer biased	Democratic, internal and external
	Central mainframe, copiers	Distributed computing and copying
Power	Formal	Informal
	Hierarchy	Networks
	Capital owners: investors	Capital controllers: key staff
3. Organisations and the collapse of structures		
Structures	Tall hierarchies	Flat matrix
	Command and control	Lead and empower
	Functions	Processes
Communication	Top down	360 degrees
	One channel, once	Multiple channels
Value and cost chain	Integrated, insourced	Fragmented, outsourced

(*Continued*)

Modern management and the new world disorder compared	Modern management	New world disorder
4. *The world of work*		
Work time	9 to 5, standardised	24/7, flexible
	Slow	Fast
	Single task	Multi-tasking
Work space	Office certainty	Hot desk uncertainty
Employment	Employment	Employability
	Standard contract	Whatever you can get
	Loyalty and sacrifice	Employee comes first
Skills	Low/technical	High: people and political
	Explicit: know what	Tacit: know how
Staff	Compliance	Commitment
	Manage sickness, absence	Manage wellness
	Salary and promotion	Recognition and status
Leadership	Traditional heroes	Team sport

Clearly, not all organisations have made the transition from modern management to the new world. There are still plenty of organisations which the revolution has yet to reach. The life insurance industry, much of the public sector and other machine bureaucracies are still stuck in the fading world of modern management. Isolated from intense competition, they do not face the same pressure to change. But when change comes, it is sudden: by then, it is too late for the legacy organisations to adapt. Elephants do not learn to dance.

The abbreviated list shows that the revolution reaches into every corner of management. In that sense it is a true revolution, because revolutions change everything. The French Revolution was not just a change of regime: it changed the calendar, introduced the metric system and introduced a new flag. It even introduced a new way of executing people efficiently, courtesy of Dr Guillotine. The management revolution has changed everything short of executing people, although even firing people has to be done very differently today from a generation ago.

An unstoppable revolution

"Stop the planet, I want to get off" was the slogan of disaffected hippies in the 1970s. You cannot stop the planet, and you cannot stop the management revolution. There are at least five drivers of the revolution which will keep it moving forward to the new world disorder.

Technology
We are inevitably dazzled by the brilliance of new technology and it is tempting to think that the revolution is all about technology. But the technology revolution has been with us for at least 200 years. In 1835, the Duke of Wellington was greatly alarmed by the advent of railways which would "only encourage common people to move about needlessly". Railways were revolutionary: they encouraged mobility, reduced the cost and increased the speed of freight, and even obliged nations to adopt a common time, or

railway time, so that timetables could be standardised. Railways were not just revolutionary in their own right: they enabled a much wider revolution of communication, mass production and mass consumption.

The technology revolution has not stopped and will not stop. Each generation thinks that it is facing exceptional technological change. In 1963 Harold Wilson, then Prime Minister, grandly announced that Britain was "to be forged in the white heat of this (technological) revolution". Looking back, it is not clear what exciting technology he was thinking about. Railways, electricity, telephones, cars, planes, nuclear power, computers and the internet can all lay claim to be the greatest change of all. The next generation will be convinced that the next round of technology innovation is greater than anything we have seen.

For management, technology means new ways of working, new ways of organising and new ways of competing.

Education
We may or may not be smarter than our ancestors, but we are certainly more educated. Fifty years ago, less than 10% of the workforce would have gone through higher education. Across the OECD, an average of 58% of young people now go through higher education. Education sustains the management revolution in at least three ways:

* Better educated employees have ever higher expectations about the nature of their work, their conditions, their pay and their prospects. Managing them can be a high maintenance activity. Managing people has moved from ensuring a compliance culture to building commitment.

- Better educated employees not only want more, they can do more and achieve more. They expect, and need, to be engaged in higher value and higher skilled activities.
- Better educated employees are shifting the balance of power from investors to workers: ownership of capital is less important than control of capital. Once the credit crunch is past, we will re-discover that the war for talent is even more demanding than the hunt for capital. The cost of talent now exceeds the cost of capital.

Affluence

We are all getting richer, even although it may not seem so in a recession. But we are far better off than our parents and our grandparents in material terms. Rising affluence changes both supply and demand.

On the demand side, more affluence creates new markets and new opportunities. Mass tourism and international travel are highly visible examples. Consumer goods which used to be luxuries for the few, from cars to fridges to computers to mobile phones, have now become necessities for the masses. Affluence enables whole new industries to be called into existence.

On the supply side, the affluent consumer becomes the expensive employee. This encourages employers to move up the value chain, to focus on higher value activities. This in turn drives fragmentation of the value chain, outsourcing and new ways of competing and of managing.

Globalisation

Globalisation, like technology, has been with us a long time. Britain's merchandise exports were 27.3% of GDP in 1890: by 1990 they had fallen to 20.6%. For the USA the equivalent figures are 5.6% and 8.0%. Advanced economies have long been globalised. What is now changing is that more countries, especially Asian countries, are entering the global economy. As a result world merchandise exports as a proportion of GDP more than doubled from 1890 to 1990 from 6% to 13%.

Globalisation reinforces the effects of affluence. On the demand side, globalisation allows for the creation of far larger markets and far more specialised segmentation of markets. Niche markets which would not have been viable at a local level become viable at a global level, allowing for ever greater innovation and competition.

Scale also accelerates technology innovation: new chip fabrication plants costing up to US$3–4 billion can only pay for themselves if they are able to serve global markets.

On the supply side, globalisation forces the pace of competition. Affluent countries have to migrate to higher value industries as low cost countries suck out all the lower value jobs which can be outsourced, from assembling shoes to managing data centres. The existence of comparative advantage has long been recognised. In 1817 the economist David Ricardo observed the possibility, but folly, of growing grapes in Scotland and of producing cloth in Portugal: globalisation allows each country to specialise in producing what it does best and then trading for the rest.

Recessions

Recessions are tough for individuals but good for progress. Recessions provide spring cleaning for the capitalist system: they help get rid of the worst (or unlucky) businesses and managers. In boom times, life is relatively easy and standards can slip. Recessions expose the weak and allow the strong to emerge even stronger when good times return.

During recessions, the forces of education, technology, affluence and education turn from benign to malign: they force managers to make difficult decisions, to change and adapt or to perish. Recessions accelerate an already rapid pace of change.

There is little reason to believe that increasing education, affluence, technology or globalisation will suddenly stop. Recessions may go, but they will come back. For all these reasons, the management revolution is not going to stop: it is going to accelerate.

As in all revolutions there are winners and losers. It pays to be on the right side of the barricades. This book is your guide to the new world disorder.

Chapter One

Strategy: From Following the Rules to Making the Rules

The theory and practice of strategy parted company some time ago. Practising managers and strategy gurus live on different planets. Occasionally they will meet at a neutral venue, such as a conference. The strategy guru will then get on stage, wave his arms and make a brilliant and inspirational speech. After which, nothing happens. The practising manager will return to his business and discover that the best predictor of next year's strategy is this year's strategy. It may be tweaked a little, but it will essentially be the same. There may be more emphasis on one channel, customer or product group. Or perhaps the pace of globalisation will be acceler- ated, or perhaps a daring CEO might make an acquisition or two. But essentially, the business will maintain roughly its previous trajectory. The exceptions to this rule are notable for being excep- tions, not the rule. WPP was a shell company which made super- market trolleys before it became the world's largest advertising company. Nokia has its roots in forest products. But if you look at the components of the Dow index, you will find all of them would be recognisable to an executive from the same company 10 years ago. Strategy theory is in danger of becoming one of the great victims of the management revolution. This is probably a good thing. Strategy theory is at best irrelevant to many companies, and at worst it is positively dangerous. The practice of strategy may be duller and more difficult than the glib answers from the gurus. But practice trumps theory every time. In this chapter we will look at why strategy theory is collapsing under the weight of its own contradictions. And then we will look at the practice that is emerging to replace it. First, we have to discover what strategy is. For many managers "strategy" simply means "important". It is often used to justify something for which there is no other justification. It is little more than puffery, for instance:

- "This strategic IT initiative ... which costs $100 million ... is essential to the survival of the firm" is a way of saying that the IT project has no financial business case to justify it.
- "Strategic Human Capital Division" is a grand way of referring to the Personnel Department.
- "This strategic programme ..." means that the speaker thinks it is important, even if no-one else does.

Strategic should mean more than "important". In truth, everyone has a different definition of strategy, which they defend with great vigour. A working definition might be something like this:

- "Optimise the role and resources of the firm to realise its vision."

This definition raises the basic strategic issues such as:

- Where should we play in the marketplace, against whom (if anyone)?
- Where do we focus our limited resources?
- How do we configure our internal and external value chain?
- What is the best way of serving our market, economically and competitively?
- Do we need to acquire, make alliances or divest to achieve our goals?

It is against this definition we will test both the theory and practice of strategy. And we will test strategy theory against three criteria:

- Does it consistently explain past successes and failures?
- Does it consistently predict future successes and failures?
- Does it prescribe accurately what organisations should do in future?

A theory which can explain, predict and prescribe is going to be very useful to managers. As we shall see, most theory fails on at least one or two of the criteria.

Strategy theory

The theory of business strategy has gone through two major phases: the classical era and the modern era. Both eras are children of the Enlightenment and of modern management: they seek universal laws which can transform average businesses into great businesses. They offer comforting simplicity in a complicated world. If they worked, that would be good. But the strategic medicine on offer is as reliable as the medicine sold by quack doctors in the Wild West. They are simplistic formulas which are weak in theory and dangerous in practice. We are now entering a third era of strategic thinking, which requires real thinking not just dumb application of an unsound formula. This is the post modern era in which there are no universal and eternal rules of success: there is only what works for each firm in the context of its time and its market. The best success formulas are discovered in practice, not designed by clever analysis.

The classical era

The classical era of strategy theory was in the true spirit of the Enlightenment. Professors, gurus and consultants all searched diligently for the empirical laws of strategy which could explain and predict the success and demise of different organisations. And they all had some success. At the heart of classical strategy are two closely linked theories:

- Porter's Five Forces analytical framework
- The BCG growth/share matrix.

In 1979 Michael Porter wrote "How competitive forces shape strategy" in the Harvard Business Review. It showed that the economic success or otherwise of a firm was dictated by five forces:

- Competitive rivalry within the marketplace
- Threat of new entrants
- Bargaining power of suppliers
- Bargaining power of buyers
- Threat of substitute products.

Nowadays, this would be called a BFO: a Blinding Flash of the Obvious. A company which faces intense pressure on all five forces is going to struggle to be more profitable than a firm which faces little pressure on all five forces. Even more modern theories, such as Blue Ocean Strategy, (Kim and Mauborgne) hark back to Porter: they argue that we should create new uncontested market space. "Blue Ocean" is a fancy way of saying what Porter said 30 years ago: compete where the competitive forces are weakest. Generally speaking, this is a good idea, unless you are an established business in an established market. The idea that an engineering company should reinvent itself as a specialist finance company, or as a creative dot.com, makes sense only to the guru inspiring jaded executives at the big conference. The Five Forces analysis offers neither hope nor insight to executives who are fighting for survival in a heavily contested industry.

The strength and the weakness of "Five Forces" is that it is fuzzy. You cannot easily quantify any of the forces. It does not lend itself to a stunning equation such as $e = mc^2$. This makes it hard to either prove or disprove. It is even difficult to define at what level the analysis should take place. Ferrari and Fiat compete in the auto industry, but arguably do not compete against each other and face very different competitive forces in their market segments. Definitions aside, Five Forces can be very dangerous when applied in practice. It leads to a self-defeating and self-fulfilling prophecy that certain markets are not worth contesting because they are so intensely competed. Household detergents, the oil industry and supermarket retailing are all intensely competed with intense buyer pressure. That does not stop Procter & Gamble, BP or Wal-Mart from being profitable. The steel industry does very poorly on the Five Forces analysis: intense rivalry, high threat of substitutes, intense buyer pressure. It would take a brave person to tell Lakshmi Mittal that steel is not an industry worth going into: he has become a billionaire by building up Arcelor Mittal. Nor does the Five Forces industry give any insight as to how to succeed in such industries. Nucor has done relatively well by having an innovative business model based on mini-mills and recycling steel. For a practicing manager in an industry, Five Forces is profoundly unhelpful. To be told that you are in an unattractive industry leads to the obvious question: so what? Should we all disappear and set up a dot.com or a vegan farm in Vermont? Nor does it give us any insight as to how we can make the most of the industry in which we are.

The Five Forces found more precise definition in the BCG (Boston Consulting Group) growth/share matrix and its close relative, The GE (General Electric) grid. BCG looked at the relative market share of a company versus the relative market growth of the industry. Share relative to competition was used as a proxy for the competitive strength of the firm. Growth of the market relative to nominal GDP was used as a proxy for the attractiveness of the market. The GE grid used similar dimensions, but allowed for a more qualitative assessment of the attractiveness of the market and the competitive position of the firm.

Both the GE grid and the BCG matrix focused on the individual firm, not just on the industry as a whole. They were also used as diagnostic and prescriptive tools. Depending on where each business was placed on the grid, it was to be treated differently as shown in Figure 1.1 on page 34.

Before we bury the consultant's world of the two by two matrix (or three by three if you are very sophisticated), let us first praise it. First, the growth share matrix is supported by research and

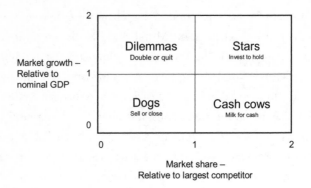

Figure 1.1 BCG growth/share matrix

experience. Market leaders find it easier to generate cash than market followers. This is not surprising. In any business, there are significant fixed costs: the higher volume business (the market leader) gets more revenue for the same fixed cost. Even today, that is a good recipe for better profitability. The problems start when the matrix is used as a substitute for thinking, not an aid for thinking. Then the framework becomes a prison, and a very dangerous prison, for anyone who goes there. Below is a classic output from a portfolio analysis: it arrayed all of the businesses of a food company on the BCG matrix. The size of each circle is in proportion to the sales of each business unit.

When we adjusted the analysis for the requirements of the GE grid, the results were broadly similar. The results illustrate three of the most common problems with such analysis:

1.   There were huge problems of definition: were cafes one business or separate businesses for separate chains? Were milling

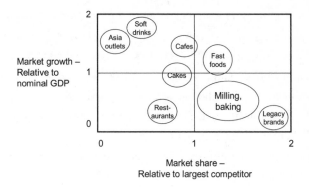

Figure 1.2 BCG Growth/share matrix for a foods group

and baking different or the same? What was the relevant market to compare them against?

2. The results tended to cluster around the middle of the chart (for the sake of clarity, the figure has spread them out further than the actual analysis). This made potentially huge decisions rest on very minor changes in either the data or the definitions: it was a recipe for arguments and politicking.

3. The prescriptions suggested by the analysis would have killed the patient, not cured it, as we shall see below. Clearly, it is the third problem which is the greatest. The analysis suggested that milling and baking should be quietly run down for cash, while the business focused on becoming a world beater in frozen foods and perhaps a couple of other high growth businesses. But the business was essentially based on milling and baking: that is what they knew how to do best. The more insightful prescription was to invest even more in milling and baking, and to take over other milling and baking operations. Since everyone in the industry was doing the same analysis,

they were more than pleased to dump their milling and baking businesses at low cost. Meanwhile, we sold off the niche businesses in cafes, frozen foods, Asia and the like: these commanded huge prices because everyone who was following the orthodox strategy thought that they should be investing in such high growth businesses. As a result, the baker raised large amounts of money to invest in more baking operations: it improved its operations, market position and cash flow.

Even more radically, another competitor realised that all the major companies were rationalising their brand line ups and wanted to dump their declining legacy brands. It built a large portfolio of such ageing brands, and built expertise in sustaining them: they could give them more care and attention than the large FMCG (fast moving consumer goods) companies.

The experience of these two companies hints at the fatal flaw in classical strategy: it is self-defeating. If one firm follows a strategy it may be strategically brilliant. If everyone follows the same strategy you have competitive suicide. Entire industries have shown that they are highly capable of following suicidal collective strategies. Over the period of 1968 to 2005 ICAO estimate that the global airline industry has lost $4 billion. Although there are some winners, such as the low cost airlines and some oligopolies, the rest of the industry operates a broken model from which they cannot escape. Other industries get caught up in the hype of the newest idea like the dot.com boom. They think it will be different this time and that everyone will succeed. The madness of crowds affects the boardroom as much as the post room. Four examples will make the point:

1. *Financial Service deregulation UK 1986 (Big Bang):* Until 1986 only four firms were allowed to make markets in UK government bonds. After deregulation everyone did the same analysis which showed that this would be a very attractive market. 26 players entered the market, and they all lost money for years: too many competitors chasing too little business. Two firms stood against the fashion rush: Schroders and Lloyds avoided the market and became highly profitable at least partly as a result.

2. *Telco 3G licences (UK):* after a marathon 150 rounds of bidding five firms won 3G telco licences in the UK at a cost of £22.4 billion, way beyond the expected outcome of about £5 billion. The price paid came to over £500 per adult in the UK. This was a good example of the winners' curse: they all managed to overpay significantly in their desperation to win.

3. *Dot.com mania 1998–2000:* Dot.com became dot.bomb as the world discovered that the laws of competition had not been suspended for the internet. The tech heavy NASDAQ has essentially been in a bear market for the nine years since the bubble burst.

4. *Global Financial Services (again):* 2008–2009 credit crunch. Financial services firms thought they had discovered the secret of alchemy: they could lend sub-prime then package up the debt and diversify away the risk. They all made the same, flawed assumptions about risk and diversification. Bankers thought they could make a jewel from a pile of junk through the miracles of diversification and financial packaging. We now know the truth: junk is junk and a pile of junk is not a jewel; it is more junk. The risk did not disappear: the risk bubble grew until it burst and led to global recession.

In each case, very smart managers, bankers, consultants and entrepreneurs were doing the same industry analysis to persuade themselves that they had found a gold mine. It turned out to be fool's gold. They were not digging for gold: they were digging a grave for their shareholders' money.

Let's see how classical strategy tools measure up against the three tests outlined earlier in this chapter:

1. Does it consistently explain past successes and failures? On average, classical strategy diagnostics help sort winners from losers. But on average a human being is 51% female and has less than two eyes. Much of the real interest is in the outliers: firms which succeed in spite of the predictions of classical diagnostics. We can learn as much about strategy from the outliers as we can from the mainstream. As a set of theories, classical strategy suffers from the problem of apples falling upwards: there are too many exceptions to make the theory sound.

2. Does it consistently predict future successes and failures? At an industry level, classical strategy gives an idea of which industries are likely to be profitable. At a company level, it predicts that leaders will remain leaders and laggards will remain laggards. This is broadly true, but the exceptions are numerous and as interesting as the mainstream.

3. Does it prescribe accurately what organisations should do in future? This is the main failure of classical strategy. It either gives no insight as to what managers should do (Five Forces) or it gives potentially the wrong insight (BCG grids). Many of the most successful strategies are creative and owe nothing to the mechanistic prescriptions of classical strategy.

Modern strategy

In the last 20 years there has been a revolt against classical strategy. At the head of the revolution was CK Prahalad, who nurtured a generation of revolutionary followers such as Gary Hamel, Chan Kim and Venkat Ramaswamy who all have Michigan Business School in their backgrounds. The manifesto for modern strategy came in two Harvard Business Review articles on Strategic Intent and Core Competence. Over the years, these ideas have been watered down. Consultants and managers now use "Strategic Intent" as a grand way of referring to a target, and "Core Competence" as a grand way of referring to anything the firm may be good at doing.

The ideas that CK Prahalad and his acolytes developed were powerful and original. They rejected the highly mechanistic view of the world which Porter and BCG implied. They noticed that many of the big strategic winners were firms which on any rational basis should not have succeeded.

The Introduction showed how the industrial landscape has been changed by upstarts who appeared out of the competitive wilderness. CNN, Canon, Dell, Toyota and SouthWest Airlines all took on heavily entrenched incumbents and succeeded.

Thirty years ago they were competitively irrelevant. The challengers had none of the resources, market power, financial muscle or technology of the incumbents. On any rational strategic analysis they stood no chance of succeeding against the incumbents. And yet in every case the challengers found ways of undermining and overthrowing the incumbents. Also, none of the incumbents relied on the internet revolution: their success was not about technology, it was about management. Clearly, there was something to be learned from these stories.

The answer that CK Prahalad came up with was Strategic Intent and Core Competence. Each of the challengers was very focused on a highly ambitious goal (strategic intent) and carefully built up all the market and technical capabilities required to achieve the goal (core competence). As an example of core competence he would show how Honda's expertise in motors allowed it to play in the markets for everything from snowmobiles, to outboard motors, motorbikes, lawn mowers and small cars.

Although the theory sounds exciting, there are three reasons why the reality does not live up to the hype:

1. *None of the examples of strategic intent and core competence used Strategic Intent or Core Competence.* The theory was retrofitted onto reality. Canon, Xerox, Honda and Komatsu did not use Strategic Intent and Core Competence, although they are held up as examples of it. This is not necessarily bad: an apple does not know about gravity but it still obeys gravity when it falls. Unlike apples, most managers have thought and intention, so we should be cautious about theories based on examples where the theory was not used. There was no systematic test of companies using strategic intent versus a control group not using it. In the absence of such a test, the theory looks like special pleading and story telling more than anything which a professor should put his name to. The theory lacks intellectual rigour or credibility.

2. *There are plenty of other reasons why the challenges succeeded.* The quality movement can claim that the quality revolution was at the heart of the success of Toyota and Honda: a radical re-engineering of the value chain drove Dell's success and that of Ryanair and Southwest followed one of the oldest strategies of all, cheap and low cost.

3. *Strategic intent and core competence are not easily replicated by management.* In practice, they are used as rallying calls to get managers to accept tough goals and to focus limited resources better. These are worthy objectives, but scarcely revolutionary.

A second generation of modern strategy arrived with CK Prahalad's protégé, Chan Kim. Chan Kim, assisted by Renée Mauborgne, introduced Blue Ocean Strategy to the world. There were two core ideas at the heart of Blue Ocean Strategy. First, it is better to seek out uncontested territory (Blue Oceans) rather than compete in highly contested existing markets (Red Oceans). As a way of finding uncontested territory, managers were to draw value curves of what their customers really wanted and what their competitors offered and then re-engineer their competitive offering to deliver maximum value at minimum cost. This is called value innovation and leads to companies deciding which value factors can be reduced or eliminated, raised or created entirely afresh.

Their examples include Formule 1 hotels (which are very cheap), Cirque du Soleil and Dyson vacuum cleaners. Yet Blue Ocean Strategy suffers from the same three problems as strategic intent and core competence

1. The theory has no intellectual validity: there is no control group, no systematic test of the theory. Attractive but selective stories of business success are just that: attractive, but selective. It is as valid to read a business leader's autobiography and try to follow those stories of success. Richard Branson, Jack Welch and many others are not shy about offering advice and giving insight into their personal brilliance.

2. The firms they studied did not use Blue Ocean Strategy and succeeded for many other reasons. Dyson's vacuum cleaner was not a product of analysing and designing value curves. It was the product of analysing and designing vacuum cleaners so that they work better. Theories are retrofitted onto past success.

3. Blue Ocean Strategy is not easily replicated by management. China Mobile CEO Wang Jianzhou talks about China's hinterland as a classic "blue-ocean market", but that is less a matter of strategic brilliance and more a case of regulatory permission and licensing arrangements. Legacy firms find it hard to create completely new ways of competing in new markets: Blue Ocean describes how new entrants compete more than it helps legacy firms.

Modern strategy is a revolution which is failing. It is long on hype and hope, but short on results or practicality. Simplistic formulas are good business for gurus, speech makers and consultants. They are attractive, but unhelpful, for managers. This leaves managers in an awkward spot. Orthodox, classical, strategy is clearly dangerous for all the reasons that the advocates of modern strategy point out. But modern strategy does not seem to offer the solution either. This appears to leave managers nowhere to go: no-one seems to have an answer to their pressing strategic challenges.

Perhaps managers are looking in the wrong direction. For a generation or more, managers have been dazzled by the brilliance of strategy gurus from Porter through Hamel to Chan Kim and beyond. As young managers they have paid a small fortune to learn the prescriptions at business schools. As senior managers they have paid a large fortune to hire the gurus and the consultants to give them the answer. And the gurus and consultants have been very persuasive: like the medicine men of the nineteenth century Wild West they have promised to cure every corporate disease from a flagging share price to drooping morale. The shock is not that anyone offers the quack medicine: the shock is that managers want to buy it.

If gurus and consultants offer the quick fix, it is tempting to take it. If you follow the latest fashion, or if you hire McKinsey, then you cannot be faulted for effort even if things go wrong. If you have not explored Blue Ocean, or whatever the latest fad may be, then you are at risk if things do not go well. Fad surfing is easy and low risk. And in practice, the consultants may do some good anyway. They will use the latest fad as an excuse to work with you. Once they have started, consultants will do what is best for you, rather than be slaves to fashion following the latest fad or formula.

Using a formula, any formula, probably leads to the Hawthorne effect: just by doing something as opposed to doing nothing, managers are likely to improve performance. This should not be taken as proof that the formula works: it should be taken as proof that active management is preferable to passive management. The Hawthorne effect was noted after a series of experiments at the Hawthorne works outside Chicago over 1924 to 1932. Each time working conditions were altered, productivity rose. When conditions were returned to the original state, productivity rose again. Staff were responding to the attention they received, rather than to the changed conditions.

Managers have let themselves become too dependent on the fads, gurus, consultants, formulas and quick fixes. The strategic revolution is to declare independence from the whole strategy industry. Originally, the strategy industry supported and helped managers. Now the industry has become a monster which is always looking for new clients on which to feed its insatiable appetite for revenues. The consulting partner's secondary objective is to help you: the primary objective is to meet the fees and earnings goals of the consulting firm.

Strategy frameworks which were originally intended to assist management thinking have become substitutes for thinking. When frameworks become formulas, they become prisons which stop managers thinking rather than help them. Both classical strategy and modern strategy can help if they are used properly: to help the creative process rather than as a substitute for it.

Strategy in practice

In practice, the strategic process is more creative and unpredictable than the formulas of modern and classical strategy imply. To tell managers that the strategic process is creative and unpredictable is liberating, but not helpful. Instead of abandoning managers in a bog of uncertainty, it pays to help in three ways:

1.   Illustrate the variety of strategic approaches.
2.   Show how managers can be creative.
3.   Show how managers can evaluate a strategy.

Different types of strategic approach

There is no simple formula for creating a successful strategy. Different sorts of firms in different situations use different approaches. A critical difference is between incumbents and new entrants. New entrants need new approaches and can afford to be radical. They cannot afford to compete in the same way for the same markets as the incumbents. The priority for incumbents is to protect what they have and perhaps grow incrementally. They will try to raise barriers to entry. For both incumbents and new entrants, competitive advantage can focus on the customer franchise, competitive weaknesses, product innovation or excellence or process efficiency and cost leadership. There is a huge range of ways to compete and succeed. The table below summarises the main types of approach:

	Incumbents: raise entry barriers, create multiple layers of advantage	New entrants: asymmetric warfare, new competitive space
Customer focused	Branding, inertia: P&G, Unilever	Exploit new market space: Facebook, Cirque du Soleil
Competitively focused	Network, scale economies: Utilities, phone companies, Microsoft, Google	Exploit segments ignored by incumbents: Komatsu, Canon
Product focused	Internal innovation machines: Pharmaceuticals, aero engines	Better mousetraps: Dyson, Freeplay
Efficiency/ economically focused	Learning curve, scale economies Auto manufacturing, banks	Re-engineered costs: Discount airlines, Dell

The purpose of this framework is to show the variety of strategic approaches which can work. It is not intended to be a strategic formula which managers slavishly follow. The whole point is that there is no single recipe for strategic success. New entrants, in particular, need to find new ways of competing if they are to succeed against the incumbents. David did not beat Goliath by fighting on the same terms as the giant. He changed the rules of the game by using a sling shot instead of his fists: he was adopting asymmetric warfare and strategy without the help of any fancy theory. The prospect of death can be a great spur to creativity.

Within this framework, there is a deeper choice to be made. The choice is between root or branch strategy. Branch strategy is incremental: it is based on muddling through. Root strategy is about step change and challenging the fundamental logic of the firm and the industry. Most firms, most of the time, prefer branch strategy. They muddle through. The best predictor of next year's strategy is this year's strategy, with the odd tweak here and there. This is a much maligned approach, but it works very well in stable industries. The risks are low and it follows the first imperative of most firms: defend what you have. When a new entrant comes in with a root strategy, with asymmetric competition, the branch style firm often does not have the capacity to change. They continue to find that defending what they have is preferable to fundamental change. By the time the need for fundamental change is accepted, it is often too late.

How to be creative strategically

When managers are told to be creative they tend to break out in a cold sweat. It conjures up images of brainstorming sessions where you are asked to imagine what sort of car or dog you or your product would be if it was a car or a dog. Fortunately, you do not have to think about cars or dogs to be creative. There are at least four ways in which to be strategically creative:

Copy an idea

Copying doesn't sound creative, but it is effective. Take someone else's idea and scale it up or copy it into another market. Ryanair essentially copied SouthWest airlines and imported the discount airline model into Europe. The idea was there for all to see: Ryanair had the wit to take the idea up. Ray Kroc bought up an idea for fast food developed by Dick and Mac McDonald: their restaurant at San Bernadino, which was based on production line methods, also inspired James McLamore (Burger King) and Glen Bell (Taco Bell). Copying is highly effective: the market research and feasibility has already been done which reduces both the risk and the investment. There are great ideas out there today, for anyone who has the courage to copy them and build them.

Solve a problem

Creativity is not just about blue sky thinking. It is, essentially, problem solving. The tougher the problem, the more creative the solution is likely to be. Dyson wanted to solve the problem of vacuum cleaners having dirty bags which reduced suction as they filled up. 5,127 prototypes later he had finally designed his world beating vacuum cleaner. Dyson's example shows that solving problems is not easy.

The tougher the problem, the more creative the solution has to be. For instance, when I first started work with P&G, Jurgen had been given his big break: he was to become a country head for the detergent manufacturer. His brief was simple: make the country profitable and become market leader. The brief was simple, the solution was difficult. The market leader had about 60% market share with one product, Whizz. Jurgen's product (Sudso) typically had about 40% market share. Whizz benefited from economies of scale: manufacturing unit costs were lower and its advertising budget went much further. Because Whizz was the brand leader, the retail trade supported it better and normally offered it at a discount to Sudso, even although the trade bought both products at the same price. Every time Sudso tried something, Whizz could either outspend it on advertising, or beat it on price. Sudso lost money, Whizz made money.

Jurgen's solution was radical. He ignored the scale economies by launching a series of niche brands to attack Whizz. One premium detergent was for heavily soiled clothes and another for delicate woollens; a discount brand was launched to undercut Whizz; another offered fabric conditioning as well as cleaning. Suddenly, Whizz had nowhere to go: it could not attack all the brands on all price levels at once. So it was cannibalised by all the niche products. And if Whizz's owners launched their own niche products they would simply cannibalise Whizz further and destroy its scale economies.

Jurgen's solution worked, at great initial cost. It was creative problem solving that would not have come from following any of the strategic formulas of classical or modern strategy.

Experiment

Strategic innovation rarely follows an entirely logical path. The dot.com boom was an orgy of innovation, most of which failed. Webvan and Boo.com blew billions of dollars in developing faulty models for grocery and clothes retailing respectively. It took a long time to discover that paid search, not banner advertising, was the way to monetise eyeballs in on-line search: Google emerged as the winner. Experimenting with large amounts of shareholders' money tends to be a way of losing money fast. Many of the best concepts start with a good idea, not with money. Dell started with a simple idea borne of desperation: build computers to order. At one stroke this removed the need for stocks, fire sales, sophisticated forecasting and large amounts of working capital. Many great business ideas are discovered, not designed. This implies that there is an element of randomness, of luck, in creating a world beating strategy.

Get lucky

Luck is important. For instance, Lloyds Bank decided to launch a bid for Standard Chartered which had global reach. Lloyds used its in-house investment bank, which managed to lose the bid by a wafer thin margin. Enraged, the CEO decided to abandon its investment banking and global ambitions: instead he focused on domestic acquisitions in the UK. It was a stunning strategy which led to Lloyds becoming one of the most profitable banks in the world. It was successful, but not what he had originally intended.

In aviation, Richard Branson set up Virgin Atlantic as a successor to the ill fated Laker Airlines which went bust. Virgin was also a discount airline with a very small upper class section for Branson and his music industry friends. It was not a sustainable economic model. But word spread about the fantastic (but small) upper class, and soon enough Branson found he had to expand it. Eventually, it became the main profit driver of the business and enabled him to succeed where Laker had failed, because he focused on premium traffic, not just discount traffic.

Of course, luck is not random. You have to seize the moment. Luck only comes to those who look for it. Equally, even the most creative and successful businesses find it hard to be lucky consistently. Few businesses and few lottery players hit the jackpot more than once. Google hit the jackpot with paid search: since then they have invested massively in a range of offerings from Google Maps, Street View, Google Earth, Google docs. These may enhance the core offering, but they are notable for not creating a revenue stream to equal the paid search business. Other breakthrough businesses such as eBay, Amazon, Dell and Skype have found a second breakthrough very hard. If there is a formula for innovative success, it seems to work at most once per firm.

How to develop a strategy

None of the strategic stories illustrated above fit into a neat formula. And that is the point about strategic formulation. You cannot start with a strategy manual at page one and then emerge at page 276 with a world beating strategy. This is good news for management. Managers are not slaves to someone else's formula. Managers have the freedom and responsibility to create their own future.

Strategy is a battle for ideas, and good ideas do not come from simplistic formulas. Good ideas come from seeing the world from different perspectives and challenging orthodoxy. Many of the best ideas do not come from management themselves: they come from customers, suppliers and staff. This means that the role of the manager is changing. Bosses do not have to be the brains of the business. Their job is not to do all the thinking for the firm, because in the knowledge economy no-one has a monopoly on knowledge or wisdom. The job of the strategist is to harness the wisdom, knowledge and experience of the customers, suppliers and staff to discover the solution.

The process of strategy development is messy. Typically it will consist of four elements:

Multiple perspectives
This is the natural habitat of the business school case study and the strategy consultant's case interview method. Take a problem and look at it from every angle. Asking the right questions is the only way of finding the right answers. Some of the right questions include:

- Economic perspective: how do we make money in this market? Which market segments are most profitable for us? What are the economics and scale effects of this market?
- Competitive perspective: how do our competitors make money? Which segments are they strongest in? Which segments do they overlook?
- Customer perspective: what do customers really want? What is our value proposition, our competitor's value proposition and what does our customer value? How much does it cost to acquire, serve and retain different sorts of customers?
- Channel perspective: how do we and competition go to market? Which channels do we use? Are there alternatives? What are their economics?
- Resources perspective: what technology, capabilities, rights can we exploit ourselves, or with our suppliers and through alliances and acquisitions? Where can we best focus our limited resources or find more?

When you ask these questions, be patient. Experience shows that 19 out of 20 questions may lead to a dead end. They are a waste of effort. But the twentieth question may be the one that generates the insight. Most great strategies are built on one simple insight: finding the simple insight can be very difficult.

Multiple approaches

This is where the various strategy formulas are useful. Value curves, strategic intent, BCG grids, Porter's Five Forces, SWOT analyses and more will all give different insights as to what is possible and what needs to be worked on harder. Use them to provoke thinking, not as a substitute for thinking.

Endless iteration

No individual has a monopoly on truth or insight. But the chances are that each person holds one piece of the strategic jigsaw which you are putting together. This process of talking through ideas takes time and effort. Within it, there are two traps. In many firms the process of strategic debate is not about finding the best way forward for the firm. It is about finding a consensus which minimises the risk for all the managers involved in the process. Consensus building rarely leads to breakthroughs. The purpose of the discussions is not to find a consensus: it is to find the insight that takes the firm to the next level of performance. Use of consultants and strategy formulas is another way of minimising risk, building consensus and avoiding insight. In these discussions, many managers will want to prove how clever they are by finding all sorts of problems, objections and challenges to any ideas. These challenges are politically and emotionally draining. These managers are very good at killing good ideas and preventing insight or progress. But they can also be used to test, push and develop an emerging idea even further.

Rapid testing of ideas
Some ideas can be tested through market research, although this can be a huge bear trap (see the chapter on marketing). The bear trap is that consumers often say what they think they ought to say, and their comments are constrained by what they know. They will not imagine the future for you. Innovative market research can avoid these bear traps, but the best research of all is marketplace experience.

Conclusions

Great strategy is normally very simple, but achieving simplicity is very hard. The simplistic formulas of the past are both flawed and dangerous. When managers ride the wave of orthodoxy, they sink or swim with the fortunes of the industry. Very few firms show that they can consistently swim against the fortunes of their industry. To become leaders, firms cannot follow orthodoxy. They have to be different in a relevant way.

Strategy differs greatly between new and established firms. New firms have to fight asymmetric battles: they cannot afford to fight on the same terms as the more powerful incumbents. These breakthrough strategies are often discovered, not designed. They come from seeing and solving a problem, from playing with products, from listening to customers. They succeed with a mix of luck and courage from the founders. Established firms are more risk averse. Instead of breakthrough strategies, they focus on defending what they have and then growing incrementally. They muddle through, reacting to threats and opportunities as they emerge.

Whether strategy is breakthrough or incremental, it does not rely on the simplistic formulas and formal processes of consultants and gurus. It is not about a few brilliant brain boxes designing the future on a PowerPoint presentation. The role of the manager is no longer to be the brains of the business. Managers need to liberate and harness the talent of the customers, suppliers and staff to discover and implement strategy. This is a world which is far more exciting, and dangerous, than the top down world of tired strategic formulas.

Chapter Two

Marketing: From Selling Benefits to Selling Dreams

From kings putting their faces on coins to potters putting their mark on their goods, people have understood the value of branding and promotion.

In the early days of the industrialisation, producers recognised that brands gave consumers an assurance of product quality. In the 1850s William Procter and James Gamble started putting a symbol of the moon and stars on their shipments of candles and then of soap. The trademark helped dockhands recognise their products. It also gave consumers reassurance that the soap and candles would be of a reliable quality. From those early days, good marketing was not about puffery and fancy advertising. It was a mark of product quality. Marketing is the glue which connects the product to the consumer: it encompasses product design, creating a compelling value proposition for customers, product quality, logistics and availability as well as activities such as promotion, pricing and advertising.

Since then, marketing has moved on. The birth of modern marketing coincided with the rise of radio and television. Early drama series on radio became known as soap operas because they were sponsored by soap manufacturers like Procter & Gamble and Unilever. Radio and television gave these companies an ideal platform for communicating with their mass markets in an economic fashion. Given the costs of advertising, considerable effort was put into working out how to optimise advertising spending: which brands would benefit most, which messages worked best, which audiences listened to which programmes and so on. Quickly, the disciplines of modern marketing emerged.

In the early days, marketing was referred to as the four Ps or three Cs: Products, Price, Promotion and Place or Customers, Competition and Channels. These simple alliterations focused on the most important activities of marketing. Non marketers observed that the four Ps omitted any mention of profit, and the three Cs omitted any mention of costs. Marketing was seen by some as a high cost and low profit activity.

Marketing is now reinventing itself again, because it has to. The old certainties of marketing are disappearing and a new world is emerging. It is a world in which marketing moves from the edges of the firm to centre stage. In a producer driven world marketing was often little more than an afterthought: it was a separate department which promoted the products of the firm. The shift of power from producers to the consumer means that marketing can no longer be an afterthought: it needs to be at the heart of how the firm thinks and operates. At the same time as becoming more important, it is also becoming more complicated. Fragmentation of media, channels and customers makes it harder than ever to manage a brand image well. And all the time customers are becoming more informed, more demanding and they have more choice. This is a challenge not just to marketing, but to the whole firm.

The reinvention of marketing has at least four strands, which are all connected:

Traditional marketing	Marketing reinvented
Sell benefits	Sell dreams
Research opinions	Research behaviour and attitudes
Producer push	Co-create with customers
Mass media	Fragmented media

From selling benefits to selling dreams

Looking back at old advertising is like entering a time warp. For a start, TV commercials were so s-l-o-o-w. Sixty-second commercials were standard, 90-second commercials were fairly common. Now, 30 seconds is normal. 90 seconds seems like an eternity for two housewives to be talking about the miracle of Tide washing clothes. And all the advertising was focused on the benefits of the product. For instance, in the UK, different detergents had different benefits focused on different market segments:

- Ariel for tough stains, using its biological formulation.
- Daz for white clothes like shirts, using its special blue speckle.
- Dreft for delicate fabrics, using its non biological base.

This was simple. It was also devoid of any creativity, so it was much hated by advertising professionals. But it had one redeeming quality: it worked. There are still categories where marketing is based on selling benefits. If you buy a painkiller, you want to know which one delivers the most pain relief fastest with the fewest side effects. But increasingly, it is becoming harder to either sell or buy on the basis of benefits. With nearly 50 000 products in a supermarket, no shopper has the time to weigh the relative merits of each and every product. Producers have to give consumers an easy way to short-cut a long process of rationally evaluating each and every product in the supermarket.

Even in high ticket items, consumers find it very difficult to evaluate different offerings. Customers find it difficult even to compare computers rationally. Consumers are not comparing just product features: processor, memory, speed, software, graphics and screen already give a bewildering variety of options. They are also comparing choices about finance and payments, delivery, warranties and insurance. With so much choice it becomes nearly impossible to make a fully informed rational decision. Often, consumers prefer less choice: it makes comparisons easier and reduces the risk of regret. If there are too many choices, consumers always fear that somehow, somewhere, they missed the best choice. In practice, consumers are not just buying a product, they are buying a story. In the case of buying a computer, they all want to have a story which shows that they were smart buyers who got a good bargain. They do not want to be embarrassed when they talk to family and friends who might tell them of a better deal elsewhere. Smart marketing and selling of computers is geared to persuading consumers that somehow they have got a special deal which suited their particular needs.

If the purchase of computers is not a completely rational process, then it is no surprise to find that few other categories are completely rational buying processes. People buy stories as much as they buy products. A strong brand offers the right story. Effective marketers understand what sort of story they need to build around each product. In many cases, the story is about the consumer as much as it is about the product. This stands traditional marketing on its head. Instead of extolling the virtues of the product, sell a dream which reinforces the consumer's actual or desired self-image. The product is simply part of the consumer's identity. This is fairly overt in beauty products and perfumes where the dream takes centre stage.

The business of selling dreams is never clearer than in the auto market. There are clearly plenty of rational ways in which to choose between cars: economy, safety, size, price, emissions, depreciation and features. Car owners will happily talk about all of this: it provides the rational cover for what is an emotional decision. A car is not just about transport: it is about identity. Salary, like death and sex, may be one of the few taboo discussion subjects left among friends and family. You cannot show off your salary, but you can show off your car. Economists call it a social good: it shows where you are in society and what sort of person you are. If you are a marketer, you can use this to your advantage. Let's take the example of selling a large off-road vehicle which is sold mainly to city dwellers. The vehicle will have some features which offer benefits to the driver but are also a part of a wider dream, as below:

Feature	Benefit	Dream
Four wheel drive	Car goes off road	Adventure
6 litre engine	Power	Macho man
High driving position	Good visibility	Be superior to others
Large size	Safe; large loads OK	Responsible parent

You can make up your own version of features, benefits and dreams for different types of car. Features of a car remain the same whoever you sell to; the desired benefits and the dreams are different for different sorts of buyer. A mother might be interested in the responsible parent dream, the father might want to recreate his days as an adventurer. No advertiser will come out and say: "This car is for wannabe macho men who pose as adventurers and think they are superior to everyone else while hiding behind the fig leaf of being a responsible parent." They do not need to say it. They will find a creative way of conveying the same message positively to their target buyers.

Contrast the dreams based marketing approach with the features based marketing approach. There are still car enthusiasts who can wax lyrical about the detailed features of their car. They can go through all the specifications: brake horse power, torque, engine size and more. As the enthusiast might put it: "The naturally aspirated 6.0-litre V12 hand-built engine produces 510 bhp (380 kW/517 PS) at 6500 rpm and 570 Nm (420 lb ft) of torque." This may be wildly exciting to other enthusiasts, but has a habit of inducing a catatonic stupor among non specialists. All the non specialist needs to know is "This car goes very, very fast and is really cool …"

Tapping into people's hopes and dreams requires a different way of thinking about market research. That is the focus of the next section.

From opinions to behaviour

The customer is not always right. Customers often do not know what they want until they are offered it. No-one asked for the internet, iPods or Ayurvedic massages until they were offered. And even when they want something they may lie about why they want it. Customers do not lie out of malice: they lie out of politeness and confusion. They will tell you what they think you want to hear. This makes researching opinions very dangerous territory indeed.

For years, Coca Cola was being hammered by Pepsi Cola. Research showed that a majority of people preferred the taste of Pepsi Cola when they were offered both drinks in a blind test. Pepsi Cola used this in its advertising relentlessly. Coca Cola did its own research and eventually came up with a formula which beat Pepsi. In 1985 Coca Cola launched new Coke, with a sweeter taste to beat Pepsi. Coke's Pepsi-killer backfired and nearly killed Coke. There was a huge backlash. Within 77 days Coca Cola had been forced to reintroduce the original version as Classic Coke. By year end, classic Coca Cola's market share was actually up as people redis-covered a brand they loved.

Coca Cola had been researching the wrong thing. They had been researching the product, which was not as liked as its rival. They should have been researching the brand and what it meant to its customers. The brand was more than just a sweet, carbonated soft drink with caramel and caffeine. Over the previous 100 years it had acquired a whole set of values around authenticity ("The Real Thing") and American, specifically Southern, culture. Ditching the product was an assault on the values of its customers.

The lesson from the Coke debacle is that people do not just buy a product or benefits (taste). They buy a set of values, they buy a dream and an identity. This is as true of big ticket items (the family car) as it is of small ticket items (soft drinks). We express who we are through what we buy. Rebellious teenagers are among the most driven consumerists when it comes to buying an identity for themselves: from their clothes to their choice of music, they try to discover and express their identity. Given the importance of values and identity, research needs to start with the customer, not the product.

Understanding how the product works with the customer can be elusive but enlightening. Often little signs give huge insights. In England, the leading dishwashing liquid by far is called Fairy Liquid. With a name like that, it has a very limited but cult like following in San Francisco. But give any brand time and it will build up its own values and identity. Going around working class homes I soon noticed that a bottle of Fairy Liquid would be visible from outside, sitting by the kitchen window. Putting the washing up liquid in the kitchen window is a bizarre habit. Except that the brand had values which were all about quality, aspiration, caring and pride in the home. If you had these values, you showed them off. If you bought a cheap dishwashing liquid, you quietly hid it from view. For a few pennies extra, Fairy Liquid proclaimed what sort of household you ran.

Understanding customers' values, identities, dreams and aspirations is not as easy as asking them if they prefer Coke or Pepsi in a blind test. Research agencies are becoming increasingly creative in working on this. The results are, occasionally, pure drivel dressed up in fancy language. You may be asked questions such as: "If your brand was a car/animal/watch/movie what sort of car/animal/watch/movie would it be?" But out of all the nonsense, you will occasionally find the nugget of insight which helps you understand where your product fits with your customers: you may avoid your version of the New Coke debacle.

Good marketers need to understand why people buy their product, or their rivals' product. They also need to understand how they buy the product and how they use it. Again, customers tend to lie out of politeness and confusion. Asking them how they buy or use a product will give you unreliable opinions: you will hear the customers' opinion of what they think they ought to say to you. Instead of asking opinions, research behaviour.

Supermarkets have ample opportunity to examine consumers' behaviour: they have the evidence of security cameras and check out tills which show exactly who buys what under what sorts of circumstances (time of day, store layout, music, heating and so forth). The result is a design optimised to help you empty your wallet fast. Both the entrance and the furthest corner of the store will have some staple products. The staples at the front may be fruit and vegetables, which serve to slow you down and start buying. At the furthest corner of the store you may find the in store bakery. In store baking is not the most cost effective way of baking bread: it is better done offsite by specialists. But the smell of the bakery will draw customers across the store. Aisle ends are reserved for special offers, to give the impression that the store is good value. Waiting at the check out you will be tempted by a few high margin but low unit cost items. If you asked customers how they want the store layout it would be very different:

- All staples near the entrance to help people do a quick shop if that is all they want.
- Special offers all near the staples to make saving money quick and easy.
- Fruit and vegetables near the check out, so they do not get crushed under other produce.
- No temptation from sweets at the check out, thank you.

Researching behaviour leads to completely different conclusions from researching opinions.

The danger of respecting customers' opinions too far became evident with one electrical goods retailer, who sold everything from cameras to computers and sound systems. When customers were asked why they had bought their goods, they gave the predictable answers: they bought because the products had the best combination of price and value. After listening to this research, the retailer decided on a price-led strategy. This simply led them into unprofitable price wars, so they changed the question and started to ask customers how they had bought, if they had bought at all. Customers were interviewed as they left the store, so that they did not have time to rationalise their decision. They were asked how many stores or websites they had visited, how many products they had compared, how much they had spent and so forth. The retailer found that the typical shopping trip was a very frustrating experience for the customer. Customers would be overwhelmed by the choice of products, services, warranties, financing, delivery and optional features. There was too much choice. After three or four stores, they would be thoroughly confused. What they really wanted was to speak to someone they could trust, who would offer them a simple choice and a good deal. A good deal simply meant something where they could brag to their family and friends that they had got a bargain by negotiating free delivery, a warranty upgrade, a special feature or whatever. Value was not objectively measured: it was an emotional requirement to not look dumb among your peers. It was about having a story to show they were smart. Armed with this insight, the retailer changed tack. It still had big red posters in the window offering a few special deals, but overall it no longer tried to be price leader on everything. Instead, it focused on the in store experience and upgraded the sales skills of staff to give customers the reassurance they were looking for.

Again, researching opinions and researching behaviour led in opposite directions: opinions led to unprofitable price wars, behaviour led to a profitable service-led strategy with reassurance around the customer's deal.

Market research has moved from being producer-centric to being customer-centric. It is a leap which many producers still feel uncomfortable with. As producers, we know and hopefully love our products and services. We want to talk about how wonderful our products and services are. But if we want to succeed, our starting point cannot be what we have and do today. We need to start with our customer, attempting to understand or imagine what they want or need. We need to see the world through their eyes, not our own prejudiced eyes. This is a 180 degree turn in our perceptions.

From producer push to co-creation
The shift from a producer centred view of the world to a customer centred view of the world has been slow but steady. From the early days of the Industrial Revolution the basic business model was "make and sell". First you make stuff, then you hope to sell it. In a world of limited choice, producers could succeed with a make and sell model. The nadir of "make and sell" could be found in shop queues in Soviet Russia, or with the in-flight service on Soviet airlines. Essentially, the producer had all the power and the consumer was privileged to be allowed to buy anything. It took a velvet revolution across Eastern Europe not just to overthrow communism, but also to overthrow the power of the producer. In the West, the revolution has been slower and quieter but equally complete.

Consumers are no longer an add-on at the extreme end of the value chain. They become part of the value chain. Instead of having a single interaction with the firm, there is continuous feedback between the customer, the firm and other customers. Power no longer resides with the producer, or even with a single customer. Power shifts from an institution to the network. This requires a different way of thinking about how firms interact with the market and how they create and offer value.

The integration of the customer into the value chain of the firm was clear from an early stage in service businesses. As customers, our experience of a holiday resort is framed not only by the quality of the hotel, beach, food and amenities. It is also shaped by our fellow tourists. If you find yourself sharing your holiday with the family from hell, it is hard to have a positive experience of even the best hotel. This has been recognised for a long time. The Titanic and other transatlantic liners enforced a strict class policy which segregated passengers into first, second and third class. This class policy is still in force on transatlantic flights. Airlines go to great lengths to keep business and coach classes apart. The business people do not want to be disturbed by the tourist family with the screaming kids. Even if space is available to upgrade passengers, airlines tend to be very careful about who, if anyone, they upgrade.

Across the retail service sector firms want the right customer mix. Bouncers behind the velvet ropes at night clubs are not just enforcing a dress code: they are helping the nightclub get the right mix of people into the club. And if the club offers half price drinks to women, it is to help make sure that they get the right gender balance. The purpose of a night club goes beyond waving your arms to loud music: it is to see and be seen with the right sort of people. The nightclub is being just as selective as any high end restaurant which enforces a dress code. The Ritz in London strictly enforces a jacket and tie policy for men, even for tea: the hotel cannot be smart and exclusive unless its clients also look smart and exclusive.

On the web, customers are explicitly becoming part of the product offering: their involvement enhances the value proposition in a way that the producer alone could not achieve. The examples are well known:

- Amazon: reader reviews have more credibility and reliability than the producers' reviews.
- eBay: vendor quality is assured partly by eBay, but also by the ranking each vendor receives from buyers.
- Wikipedia is a user generated product. Wikipedia provides the platform, users provide the content and much of the value.
- Facebook, Twitter and all the social media depend on user content with the firm, like Wikipedia, simply providing the platform for the interactions to occur.

Bricks and mortar firms are also finding it makes sense to involve the customer more in their value chain. Lego may not produce mortar, but it produces plenty of plastic bricks. It used to operate in traditional make and sell mode, until it discovered the talent and passion of its customers. They make top users into brand ambassadors who not only are evangelists for the brand, but also help guide innovation and new product development. And the Lego website now allows people to design their own product and then buy it. Lego has turned "make and sell" on its head. Now it sells the product which the customer has designed, then packages and delivers precisely what the customer wants. Producer push has become consumer pull. In Industrial Goods, GE polymers serve a large number of small producers with a wide variety of polymer grades for different usages. Inevitably, this raises all sorts of technical and production challenges which the small producers cannot answer, and which GE cannot economically serve. GE set up GE Polymerland, which is a forum where users can share experience and knowledge about how to use GE's polymers. The network can solve many of the problems: the customer experience is improved while GE gets valuable insight into how their customers work and what they need.

At its simplest, customers are now taking over part of the value chain which used to be delivered by the firm. Firms let customers serve themselves. This can be presented as "putting customers in control": more often it is a way of shifting costs from the producer to the consumer. Self-service started with supermarkets, then spread to gas stations, then to the internet and even IKEA has changed the furniture value chain by encouraging shoppers to assemble their own furniture. This is valid, but does not quite capture the richness of possibility that arises from involving customers in the whole value chain, rather than simply outsourcing part of the value chain to them.

Customers can be involved far earlier in the value chain, even to help design, develop and test new products. Google released early versions of Timeline and Similar Images specifically so that they could get user feedback and adapt both products to what users wanted, as opposed to what Google engineers dreamed about. Standard practice for most software companies is to release beta versions of their software so that users can help them identify problems and opportunities.

This new world has been dubbed "Experience Co-creation" by Venkat Ramaswamy of Michigan Business School. As with all new ideas it is at risk of being "productised" and dumbed down into another fad by consultants. The three essential characteristics of this new world are:

- Customers become part of the value chain.
- Interaction between the firm goes from a transaction to a dialogue.
- The firm provides a platform through which the customer network can operate.

The consequence of this is that the role of the marketing department is changing. Marketing used to be a stand alone department sitting at the end of the value chain, often called "sales and marketing". It existed to shift whatever the company was producing. Marketing can no longer exist with a producer push role. Marketing has to be part of a holistic marketing framework that infects the whole firm. Previously, marketing departments were focused on a simple question: "how do we maximise the potential of this brand?" Marketing now needs to answer a wider set of questions. The three key questions, identified by Philip Kotler in *Marketing Moves*, are:

- How can a company identify new value opportunities for renewing its markets?
- How can a company efficiently create promising new value offerings?
- How can a company use its capabilities and infrastructure to deliver the new value offerings efficiently?

To those three questions, we might add a fourth:

- How can a company use its customer network to resolve the first three questions?

These four questions are far removed from the 4 Ps or 3 Cs which traditionally consumed marketing. So far, most firms are struggling with this new world, and most marketing people are struggling with it as well. The old certainties are more comfortable than the brave new world. The critical four questions are not part of the everyday language of the firm. Instead, they tend to get answered on a project basis often run with consultants. This is better than nothing, but this is one part of the management revolution which still has far to run. Marketing is still in the process of reinventing itself.

Big media to fragmented media

In 2008 Americans and the British spent an average of 28 hours a week glued to their television sets. Over a life time they will spend nine years watching television. Across the OECD as a whole, people spend 22 hours a week watching television. In the past the big network channels dominated viewing figures. For instance, in 1980 the networks took 75% audience share for the prime evening news in the US. That was the year when US News World and Report asked "Is TV news growing too powerful?" It was also the year that CNN started a revolution of choice and fragmentation of the TV market. By 2008 the network channel's audience share of the evening news had declined to 28%, largely displaced by an explosion of choice through cable channels. Television used to be the big beast, now it is the big herd. It has fragmented dramatically, but remains important.

But television's crown is under threat. In the UK in 2008 TV accounted for 26% of all media spend: the internet accounted for 24.8% of all media spend and in 2009 it overtook TV media spend for the first time. The balance of media (advertising) spend is accounted for by outdoors (posters and sponsorship), newspapers and magazines, radio and cinema which gives a huge range of media choice.

The rise of the internet relative to TV changes the way firms communicate with customers. In the days of network television, advertising took a blunderbuss approach: it took a big shot at a big target and hoped that some of it would hit. It was a wasteful approach. John Wanamaker, the Philadelphia department store entrepreneur, complained: "Half the money I spend on advertising is wasted. The trouble is, I don't know which half." He was, perhaps, being optimistic. David Ogilvy, the advertising guru who started the leading Ogilvy agency, said: "99% of advertising doesn't sell much of anything." In the world of hit and miss mass media that might have been true. Targeting advertising was a crude business of matching your target customers to the viewing profile of different shows. That led to huge waste and it was very much one way communication. The internet changes all that.

The internet allows highly targeted communication: that is the power of Google's paid search platform. Advertisers know that they are only getting people who are actively interested in the goods and services. The 99% waste which Ogilvy complained about is cut dramatically. Unlike the broadcast media, the internet also allows two way communication. This is as revolutionary as going from radio (broadcast only) to telephones (two way communication). The technology changes the whole nature of the relationship between the producer and the consumer. With TV, the producer is in control. On the internet, the consumer is in control. The change has benefits for both producers and consumers:

(a) Consumers customise their own product and service. One size no longer fits all. The internet makes mass customisation a reality. You can specify exactly what sort of computer you want Dell to build for you; you can decide what combination of cable, television, internet, mobile and landline package you want when you subscribe to Virgin; you can build your own package holiday when you go to one of many on-line travel sites. This has obvious benefits to the consumer. It also gives powerful real time feedback to the producer: they know which offers work and which ones do not. They can customise their offerings accordingly. Airline booking systems constantly adjust their pricing and offers for each flight as demand changes: they maximise yield at the same time as consumers optimise their spend.

(b) Producers reduce their costs and waste. As soon as a firm moves from a "make and sell" model to a "sell and make" model, all the problems of forecasting, stock outs and fire sales disappear. And where the customer also becomes part of the make, through self-service (banks, travel arrangements, social websites) the cost to the firm is reduced even further. The internet becomes a platform around which the customer can customise the desired product or experience.

(c) The voice of the consumer becomes much more important. Word of mouth is amplified by the web. The old rule of thumb was that one bad service experience would be mentioned to 10 other people; a good service experience would be mentioned to three other people. A short excursion onto Amazon shows that a top review may be recommended hundreds of times, and it will have been read thousands of times. The web is word of mouth on steroids. Whether it is books, hotels, restaurants or local tradesmen, there is no hiding place for producers.

Consumers have ceased to be passive consumers of what the firm produces. They have become actively involved in shaping their purchase and their experience. Interactivity changes the way the effectiveness of media is measured.

The most common ways of measuring media and copy effectiveness were two fold:

- GRP (Gross Rating Points) gave a measure of media coverage: 200 GRPs might mean that 70% of the population saw the message an average of three times in a month. This is a useful indicator of media coverage, but gives no clue as to media or advertising effectiveness.
- DAR (Day after Recall) and then OAT (Off Air Testing) was much hated by advertising agencies but was a simple measure of advertising effectiveness. It measured how many people actually remembered seeing the advertising. DAR tested recall the day after the advertising. OAT simulated the same effect at much lower cost with test groups of customers. If no-one remembered the advertising, then no matter how creative and clever it was, it would not help sell any product. Advertising has to be remembered before it can be effective.

These are irrelevant measures in the interactive world, which allow for much more targeted measures. Although you know little or nothing about the demographic profile of people who use your site, you know something far more valuable about them: they are a self-selecting group who for some reason have interest in your site. The wastage of television advertising is averted. Eyeballs (number of unique visitors), click through and purchase rates give real time feedback on what works and what does not work. At its simplest level, SMEs can become their own advertising agencies. They can see clearly which pages people look at and which are ignored: they can redesign the site according to what visitors most want. From there, they can go on to build interactivity (email lists, blogs and client forums) to make their site a destination site.

The web allows firms to move from the waste of mass media to the laser like targeting of individuals. At its simplest, targeting is contextual. If you enter a search term such as "fly fishing Scotland" you will receive plenty of paid search advertisements for holidays and tuition for fly fishing in Scotland. The targeting is precise and enables even small, local firms to target customers from around the world cost effectively: niche businesses can profit from global media when the media can target customers well enough. Beyond contextual advertising, behavioural targeting is emerging. Firms such as Phorm will track users' on-line behaviour, from which a consumer's interests can be inferred and relevant ads can be shown. Contextual advertising focuses on a page; behavioural advertising focuses on the person. The privacy issues are real.

Targeting individuals, not mass markets, also has implications for profit management which will be explored further in the chapter on finance. The essential point is that when you know how much it costs to acquire a customer (because you can now target them clearly) and you know how much it costs to serve the customer, then you can understand individual customer profitability. That is not just of academic interest: it enables the firm to change the marketing mix, alter pricing, change the product to optimise profitability on a customer by customer basis. For instance, Capital One conducted 26 000 market tests for their credit cards in 2006 alone. They can estimate the projected value (NPV) of each customer depending on the customer's profile and how they applied for their credit card. This allows for fine tuning of their offering and it enables them to fine tune their service to maximise profitability and client retention. When a customer calls, their computers will identify the caller and route the caller to one of 50 options based on their most likely need, arming the service agent with at least two dozen pieces of information about the person calling. Capital One recognise that credit cards are essentially information: use that knowledge well and you have mass customisation, not mass media.

Fragmentation of media means that marketing has gone from being a one way broadcast to a mass market to a targeted dialogue with actual or potential customers. Most companies are still more comfortable with the old model. The old broadcast model allows them to control the message and follows well established formulas for developing and evaluating both the message and the media. The fragmented, targeted and interactive world may be a richer marketing environment, but it is much harder to control and manage. The rules of the new world are still being discovered as marketing reinvents itself again.

Conclusions

As power shifts from producers to consumers, so the importance of marketing grows. It is migrating away from being a separate department, often lumped together with sales, which existed only to push whatever products the firm had onto an unsuspecting public. Marketing is now central to the success of the firm: creating a viable value proposition for customers, targeting and acquiring customers through the right channels, optimising the product, pricing and profitability are all essential. This strategic marketing is not just the business of a separate marketing function: it is the business of all top management.

If marketing is interacting differently with the rest of the firm, it also has to interact differently with customers. Customers are no longer passive and anonymous recipients of products and services. Increasingly, they can be absorbed into the value chain of the firm by helping to design, develop, deliver and customise the product to their own needs. Each customer is not just part of a mass market, but can be identified and treated as an individual.

Marketing is moving from being product focused to being customer focused. Instead of starting with a product and hoping to sell it, start with the customer and understand their hopes, fears, dreams and behaviour. Then it becomes possible to target them with the products they want through the media they use. Marketing is slowly becoming more efficient, more focused and more integrated with the needs of the customer and with the activities of the whole firm.

Chapter Three

Power: Shifts to a New World Disorder

All revolutions are about power, and the management revolution is no exception.

The old order was simple. Bosses bossed and workers worked. Bosses had the brains and the workers had the hands: workers were not required to use their heads and managers were not expected to use their hands. Above the managers lay the owners of capital, the capitalists, who either went broke or became very rich. It was an uneasy order which allowed great wealth to flourish alongside grinding poverty. Power and wealth went hand in hand: the owners had the power and the money, and the workers had neither money nor power. Many places were one company towns, where there was no alternative employment and little by way of a social safety net. The coercive power of the owners, and through them the bosses, was huge.

The nature of power in business has been changing fundamentally. There have been four major shifts over the last 100 years, and there is no reason to think that these changes will halt or reverse.

1. Power has been shifting from the owners of capital to the controllers of capital, in other words from shareholders to managers. Workers no longer revolt against the owners: owners "revolt" against management if they try opposing the executive.
2. Power is shifting from producers to consumers.
3. Power is shifting from the West to the rest of the world.
4. The rewards of power have become very unevenly balanced: a caste system is emerging where skills, not ownership, have become the dividing line between those who succeed and those who do not.

Within organisations, the nature of power has changed completely: responsibility and authority no longer go hand in hand. Power is no longer given, it has to be taken. This is radically reshaping the job of the manager and the skills required for success. Understanding, acquiring and using power are essential not just for career advancement, but for making things happen. The changing nature of power within the organisation is covered further in the chapter on management.

We will explore each of four changes above and show what they mean for practising managers.

Power has been shifting from the owners of capital to the controllers of capital

Shareholders have been losing control to managers. The credit crunch has been a spectacular example of the shift of power from shareholders to managers, but it is just one in a long series of examples pointing in the same direction. It is a shift in power which was predicted by Adam Smith and which is taking us into uncharted water.

There has been uproar over the huge bonuses paid to executives of failed institutions. Politicians have called it "rewards for failure" or "privatising the gains and socialising the losses". AIG paid out $165 million in bonuses despite having to be bailed out with between $85 billion and $185 billion of taxpayers' money. That was modest compared to Merrill Lynch who forced through $3.6 billion of bonuses days before their takeover by Bank of America closed: without the takeover Merrill Lynch was bust. In the UK, the CEO of RBS was given a $25 million pension pot on the day he left the company, seemingly as his reward for helping destroy the bank.

The bankers are essentially an oligarchy. They press home the belief that they are too big to fail: the demise of Lehman Brothers gave them great power. If Lehman's collapse could bring the whole system to near meltdown, then clearly it was not possible to let any other bank fail. Once that belief is accepted, the oligarchs are in power: to save the system you have to save the banks which means you have to keep the talent which means you have to pay the bonuses. The steady flow of bankers into government ensures that attempts to reform the system are framed by the same people who caused its collapse.

There is flawed logic here: bankers have shown a consistent ability to fail in their fundamental task of allocating capital well. They have lurched from one fiasco to another: the savings and loans crisis, the sovereign debt crisis, LTCM (Long Term Capital Management), the dot.com bust and the credit crunch. The talent may be the problem, not the solution. And then there is the assumption that if they are not paid the bonuses they will all go somewhere else and earn more money, or start their vegan farm in Vermont. That the logic is flawed shows that the rewards are not about logic or reason. They are about power. Leaders are achieving entrepreneurial rewards for bureaucratic performance: they perform well when the economy is good and poorly when the economy is bad. Few are able to buck the economic trend and make a real difference. Rewards are neither for success nor failure: they are rewards for power.

Bankers have achieved huge rewards at great cost to both the taxpayer and their shareholders. Regulators have failed to control them. Worse, shareholders have failed to control them. Shareholders are highly fragmented and dispersed: it is hard for them to coordinate, control and force change. Company directors are meant to represent the interests of shareholders, but they fail to. In practice, non executive directors are a self-perpetuating, self-appointing and self-serving oligarchy. Many non executives serve on multiple boards where they are connected to each other: the network of oligarchs serves itself and has its own values and beliefs. Lord Myners, who made a large fortune in fund management, saw no problem in approving a small fortune of $25 million to the departing CEO of RBS. When you have $100 million fortune, then $25 million seems like a modest pay off. The oligarchs are simply disconnected from everyone else. They might bridle at the description "oligarch" although they would purr with delight at being called an elite. It is a fine distinction based on how far you think these people are acting in the public interest versus their own interest.

Shareholders have lost power. They normally rubber stamp appointments. On the rare occasions they object, it is regarded as a shareholder "revolt". In 2004 Michael Eisner faced a shareholder revolt over his plans for Disney's leadership. In the words of the press this "revolt" included barbed comments from "rebel" shareholders. This is significant language. Workers used to revolt against managers, and maybe employees could revolt against the owners. But to have the owners revolting against the managers shows that power has fundamentally shifted. Karl Marx predicted a revolution of the workers against the capitalists: the thought of capitalists rebelling against the workers would have been as plausible as cycling to the moon.

It is easy, but wrong, to point the finger just at the bankers. The shift in power is evident elsewhere as well. In the dot.com bust, 26 top executives from 20 firms which went bust took out $2.65 billion in compensation for having lost all their shareholders' money. They got rich failing, and if they had succeeded they would have got even richer. Managers had a one way bet on success: shareholders discovered that they had taken 100% of the risk. Where the dot.com CEOs led, bank CEOs followed. The top 10 firms in receipt of TARP funds from the American government received $244 billion of bail out money to stop them going out of business. In 2007 the CEOs of these 10 firms awarded themselves $242 million for helping their firms go bust.

This shift in power is not a surprise. The godfather of free markets saw what would happen when ownership and management became separated. Adam Smith, in *The Wealth of Nations*, observed of companies owned by absentee shareholders:

> The directors of such companies, however, being the managers rather of other people's money than of their own, it cannot well be expected, that they should watch over it with the same anxious vigilance with which the partners in a private partnership frequently watch over their own .... Negligence and profusion, therefore, must always prevail, more or less in the management of the affairs of such a company.

Adam Smith was predicting that managers would look after their own interests first, not the interests of shareholders. If Adam Smith and the evidence of the credit crunch are correct, there are some awkward consequences.

The first implication is that regulation will always be one step behind disaster. Regulators will busily address the symptoms of the banking problem, not the cause. The symptoms are things like inadequate capital ratios, poor lending practices and poor understanding of risky and complex financial instruments. The root cause of the problems is deeper: it is the shift of power to managers who run the bank primarily in their interest. That means maximising their returns and minimising their risk. Even share options are of limited use in aligning managers' and shareholders' interests for at least three reasons:

1. Share options can always be repriced, making them a one way bet.
2. Share options are an addition to already generous compensation packages: if things go wrong managers lose an opportunity but they do not lose real wealth, unlike shareholders who experience real losses.
3. The quickest way to boost the share price is by cost cutting and acquisitions which lead to more cost cutting and financial engineering opportunities. You cannot cut your way to growth and most mergers are poor value for shareholders of the acquirer. Managers' short term interests are not the same as shareholders' longer term interests.

The second implication is that we should have far more owner-run businesses. The evidence here is mixed. Professional service firms are owner run: law firms and consultancies have impressive growth and profit track records as private partnerships. But they can fail like any other firm: Arthur Andersen imploded in a month after their role in the Enron scandal became clear. Goldman Sachs was not immune from the credit crunch and had to turn itself into a bank, although arguably it suffered less than many of its publicly quoted peers. Some firms are simply too large to be private partnerships: Exxon and other oil majors and telcos require capital that is beyond the reach of even wealthy individuals acting as owner managers.

The third implication is that some banks are not too large to fail: they are too large to succeed sustainably. They are being run in the short term profit maximising interests of the managers. It makes sense for them to take excessive risk. If they succeed for a few years, they will make their fortunes. When they finally fail because the risk goes sour or the economy turns, managers still keep their fortune even if the bank goes bust and the owners lose everything. Managers and owners have different views of sustainability and risk. By the time the credit crunch becomes a folk memory, the banking industry will be heading to its next crisis.

Power is shifting from producers to consumers

Henry Ford revolutionised auto manufacturing with the Ford Model T. His aim was to "build a car for the great multitude". He succeeded greatly: over 15 million Model Ts were produced. Part of the success was in driving the price down: that meant revolutionising production (Ford introduced moving assembly lines) and value chains (he integrated all the way back to owning the forest which produced wood for the car). It also meant limiting choice. Henry Ford is reputed to have said: "Any customer can have a car painted any colour that he wants so long as it is black." GM dethroned Ford largely by offering choice. GM went beyond offering different colours. GM also offered different cars: Chevrolet, Pontiac, Oldsmobile, Buick and Cadillac. In Alfred Sloan's words, GM offered "a car for every purse and purpose". This was a revolutionary shift. Ford had succeeded with a producer-led view of success: optimise production efficiency. GM succeeded with a customer-led view of the world: give each customer a choice.

The explosion of choice has continued. The Food Marketing Institute (2004) estimates that the average number of products stocked in a US supermarket rose six fold from 1970 to 1999: from 7800 to 49 225 product lines. In such a choice rich world, producer-centric firms lose out to customer focused firms. If cash is king, then the customer is the emperor in this new world. Power and profit do not come from owning production: they come from owning the customer relationship. This puts retailers in a strong position compared to their suppliers and auto makers in a strong position relative to their suppliers. The customer end of the value chain is where the power lies. This can be seen in the mark ups achieved at each stage of the value chain.

To discover the power of owning the consumer relationship, wander down to your local Starbucks and order a cup of coffee. Then try to work out the value chain that lies behind your cup. The wholesale price of coffee is around 130 cents per pound. That will yield 30–40 cups of coffee (depending on how strong you like your coffee and how big you like your cups). That works out at about four cents per cup of coffee for the actual coffee: the farmer who produced the beans will get less than this wholesale price. But you may have paid $2–$3 for your cup of coffee. Clearly, Starbucks have added much value and cost to the process. They add enough value to turn every four cents of coffee bean into $2–$3 of revenue. The value no longer lies with the producer (farmer) it lies with the chain which owns the consumer (Starbucks).

In the PC arena, Michael Dell made the same discovery: value is close to the consumer. As a teenager, he dismantled various computers including a $3000 IBM PC. He figured out that the cost of the components was about $500. The $500 contained all the highly sophisticated design, technology and engineering for processors, memory chips and mother boards. But the value did not lie in the technology. The value lay in the final stage of the value chain: assembling the components to the requirements of the consumer and shipping it to them direct. Cutting out retailers is not cheap, but it is where 80% of the value can be captured.

In the apparel industry the retailer will typically take $30–$50 of every $100 of value. The raw material will have cost about $10 and the garment worker in Asia will receive perhaps $2–$6. The rest disappears in taxes, transport, insurance, factory overheads and profit for the garment makers. Wherever we look, most value and most costs are captured by the firm which owns the consumer franchise. Improving productivity of the garment worker by 20% has a negligible effect on the retailer's economics. Improving retail efficiency 20% has a dramatic effect on profitability for the retailer.

Not every firm can own the customer: not everyone is a retailer. An alternative way of owning the consumer relationship is through branding. The marketing chapter shows that branding is becoming even more important to survival in the new world disorder. There is an inevitable power struggle between brands and retailers. UK grocery stores have led the way in developing own label products: by 2004 they accounted for 42% market share of the categories they compete in, with over 70% market share for some markets such as ready meals. Suppliers to supermarkets face a stark choice: invest in your brand or become dependent on the whims of the supermarket. The side which owns the customer franchise has the power. The strong brands can cope with the power of the super-markets. Brands which have built up their own customer franchise, from detergents to smoothie fruit drinks, are holding on against own label products. The strongest brands can even dictate to retail-ers. Luxury goods makers such as Gucci, Ferregamo and Louis Vuitton maintain strong control over distribution, from pricing discipline to displays.

The power of the consumer is not only coming from greater choice. It is also coming from greater information. In the past, there was huge asymmetry of information between the producer and the consumer. The producer knew all about what they were producing, and would choose what they wanted the consumer to know. That is now all changing. The consumer is likely to know enough to challenge the producer and make a much more informed decision about their choices: in the past they may not even have known that they had a choice. The classic producer driven market used to be the medical profession. We would go to our doctor and the doctor would decide what was best for us: we had the problem and they had the solution. We relied on their skill and knowledge. Now patients are much more informed: they will quiz doctors, explore alternatives and will identify for themselves the best specialists to consult. Some doctors are happy with this, many are not.

Consumers used to be passive: they purchased goods and services from a limited choice provided by producers. Now they're getting active. Increasingly, the consumer voice is making producers listen and react. The consumer voice is certainly helping consumers make much more informed choices. At a simple level, customer reviews on Amazon are more highly valued than the producer's product description of the same product. Producers tell us what they want us to hear: consumers tell us what we need to hear. The voice of the consumer can be very strident and much feared. A few examples:

- GM crops have come under sustained attack by the environmental lobby in Europe, which has led to severe restrictions on GM foods, termed "Frankenstein Foods", in Europe. They may or may not be right to protest, but the power of their protest is not in doubt. They have cowed politicians into creating tight controls over GM crops.
- Sunny Delight came from nowhere to being a top drink for children in the UK. A health scare started and the product disappeared as quickly as it had appeared.
- In 1990 Perrier recalled all of its product because benzene had been traced in some of its bottles. William M. Grigg, a spokesman for the FDA found that there was no great threat: "At these levels there is no immediate hazard," he said. "The hazard would be that over many years, if you consumed about 16 fluid ounces a day, your lifetime risk of cancer might increase by one in a million, which we consider a negligible risk." There may have been no health risk, but the brand and reputation risk was huge. Perrier saved its reputation as a result of its apparent overreaction to a small problem.

More positively, the power of the consumer is being harnessed to help co-create goods and services of the future: the co-creation process has been mapped out in detail by Venkat Ramaswamy in *The Future of Competition*. The essential argument is that much greater interaction and dialogue with customers is needed to develop winning goods and services. It looks at the whole customer experience, not just at the product itself. The approach stands in contrast to the slightly old fashioned approach of *Blue Ocean Strategy*, which still relies on brain boxes doing analysis and coming up with insightful value curves. Blue Ocean Strategy still assumes that the producer produces and the consumer consumes: co-creation challenges that view. Consumers expect to have their voice heard.

Not every firm has the luxury of owning the consumer relationship. Life further down the value chain, away from the consumer, can be uncomfortable. Auto makers separate their suppliers into three tiers: Tier 1 are their major suppliers, Tier 2 supply Tier 1, and Tier 3 are the myriad smaller suppliers at the bottom of the food chain. When the auto makers catch a cold, their suppliers catch pneumonia. Faced with intense rivalry from other suppliers and depending heavily on a few major customers makes the auto suppliers very vulnerable. Not surprisingly, it is an industry which is consolidating fast. PwC estimate that between 1988 and 2015 the number of suppliers will decline from 30 000 to 2800 in what is a slow moving but dramatic revolution.

Surviving far from the consumer interface is possible. If you have the lowest cost of production (selected upstream oil companies or mining firms for instance) you will be the last man standing in any price war or market collapse. Equally, firms which have superior proprietary technology (pharmaceuticals, software) will do well. Some firms, and most of the public sector, also enjoy natural monopolies which makes life easy. The public sector is virtually recession proof. If you lack the technology, cost advantage or consumer franchise or legal monopoly, you will suffer.

Power is shifting from the West to the rest of the world

Comparative advantage is why globalisation is so attractive economically. David Ricardo is credited with developing the idea of comparative advantage in his book *On the Principles of Political Economy and Taxation*, written in 1817. The core idea is that each country should focus on what it is best at, or least bad at, producing. Adam Smith hinted at the same idea in 1776 when contemplating the improbable idea of Scottish wine:

> By means of glasses, hotbeds, and hotwalls, very good grapes can be raised in Scotland, and very good wine too can be made of them at about thirty times the expense for which at least equally good can be brought from foreign countries.

The thought of Scottish wine should be enough to convince most people of the benefits of global trade and comparative advantage. At least this is good news for consumers. For managers, comparative advantage implies greater competition from across the globe. The process of globalisation is producing another power shift, from the West to the rest of the world. The world of management is still getting to grips with this shift.

In the introduction to this book we noted that globalisation is not new. In 1890, Britain's merchandise exports were 27.3% of GDP; by 1990 they had fallen to 20.6%. Over the same period world merchandise exports had grown from 6% to 13% of global GDP. This is mainly the result of the rise of Asia and its integration into the world economy.

The rise of Asia started as a story about low costs. In some areas it still is about low costs. WalMart has effectively become the export agency for China Inc. sucking in low cost apparel, shoes and home wares: US manufacturers cannot compete on price in these categories. This is likely to be the first wave of globalisation. In the next wave China will move up to higher value, higher quality goods, challenging mature industries elsewhere. Japan started in similar fashion, producing low cost and often low quality goods after World War Two. No-one would accuse Lexus, Sony or any other Japanese car and consumer goods companies of being low quality. The rest of Asia is following suit.

The result is a shift in economic power. Chinese GDP has grown from 6% of world GDP in 1980 to 13% in 2004. That is still well behind the United States 23% share of world GDP, but the gap is closing fast. Asia, led by Japan and China, owned 31% of all outstanding US treasuries in 2008: the credit crunch will lead to increased reliance on Asian funding to support increasing government deficits, unless Americans and Europeans learn to save more and spend less. Otherwise we will rely on low paid Chinese workers lending us their money so we can buy their goods. Both sides have found this unlikely arrangement to be convenient, but it is not sustainable.

Globalisation creates huge opportunities, but at high risk. More and more jobs are tradable. Ricardo's concept of comparative advantage is as relevant as ever. Tradable jobs will tend to concentrate in the country which has a comparative advantage in that business. Much has been made of the growth of software outsourcing in Bangalore. Bangalore is a symptom of a much larger shift. In the industrial era, tradable jobs were mainly to be found in tradable industries. The result was that entire industries more or less vanished in the West. The UK's Industrial Revolution was built on coal, steel, clothing and shipbuilding. Those industries are mere ghosts of what they once were. In the new era of globalisation, even service jobs are becoming increasingly tradable. Professionals can be big winners and losers in this new world. Clearly, software has seen huge growth in India. But New York and London have benefited greatly from the globalisation of financial services.

There is little point in hiring an unskilled American worker earning $426 a week, when you can hire 10 equivalent workers in India, or one highly skilled worker in India for the same amount of money. In 2005 McKinsey estimated that there are 160 million service jobs that could be done anywhere in the world. That estimate excludes all the jobs that can be offshored in manufacturing. The potential for displacing jobs is huge. Jensen and Kletzer of the Institute of International Economics estimate that up to 50% of the workforce may be working in tradable jobs. This is made of both tradable industries (auto manufacturing, for instance) and tradable jobs (writing software).

To put the theory into practice, consider a few simple examples: the school janitor, marking school assessments, and child rearing:

- The school janitor is not in a tradable job: you cannot get your forecourt cleaned in China. But the janitor is at risk if his employer is an auto manufacturer, because that is a tradable industry which could go bust.
- Education is not a highly tradable industry, except at the highest level where there is a global market of supply (professors) and

demand (students). But marking multiple choice tests is a highly tradable job. It is a job which can be delivered electronically. If the scoring for a school in Arkansas can be delivered from Arizona, there is no reason it cannot be delivered from Asia.

- Most families would feel offended if someone suggested that they outsource child rearing to a cheap offshore centre. Employing a nanny from the Philippines who repatriates most of her earnings to her family in Manila is effectively offshoring child rearing. If child rearing can be sent offshore, most jobs can be sent offshore.

The stakes are high because tradable jobs do not disperse themselves evenly across the globe. Instead, many industries will divide between winners and losers. Instead of dispersing, industries have always had a natural tendency to cluster. This trend was first observed by the Cambridge economist, Alfred Marshall, at a time when the UK had natural clusters around china and pottery (Stoke and the Black Country) cutlery (Sheffield) and apparel (Lancashire). These were clusters which were not just nationally dominant: they were global leaders. The tendency of industries to cluster is natural: it makes the flow of goods, services, skills, ideas and innovation much easier. Once the cluster is established, it becomes self-reinforcing: more of the skills, customers, entrepreneurs and suppliers are drawn to the centre of excellence and capability. Clusters reinforce the sense of comparative advantage. Some leading clusters include:

- Financial Services: New York and London
- High Tech: Silicon Valley, California

- Diamonds: Antwerp
- Motorsport, IndyCar and Formula 1: South East England
- Jeans: Guangdong
- Software: Bangalore

The West is high cost and lazy compared to the rising Asians. Asian working hours are typically 50% longer over a year than in the West, and their pay may be 10% of what their counterpart in the West would earn. This is not a sustainable position to hold. The escape route for the West is to go to higher value added services: Europe and USA is not going to compete successfully with Asia in coal, shipbuilding or apparel any longer. But moving to higher value added services requires higher skills levels. Our prospects are mixed, at best. OECD countries, which are mainly Western, now have 30% of 25–34-year-olds who have gone through tertiary education. South Korea and Japan have already moved ahead: over 50% of the same age group have gone through tertiary education. This is the age group which represents the future competitiveness of each nation. India and China are lagging relatively, with 8% and 5% respectively of 25–34-year-olds having gone through tertiary education. Although the proportions are small, the numbers are vast given that China and India have a combined population of over 2.5 billion, compared to 0.7 billion in the USA and Europe. China alone currently has 20 million students who will become their skilled workers and managers of the future.

For management, globalisation makes the world more exciting, dangerous or complicated depending on your point of view. It is more exciting because it creates more opportunities both professionally and for the firm. It is more dangerous because in a globalised world both firms and managers' jobs are at risk from competitors around the world. It is more complicated because managing a global value chain is far harder than managing a local value chain.

Technology has greatly assisted the business of managing globally. From the basics of email and video conferencing through to global enterprise software, the basic glue of working without borders has been put in place. But technology is not the whole answer. For many managers, globalisation is not part of the day to day reality of business. For instance, Aviva owns insurance operations in both Iowa and Norwich, England. A claims manager or insurance underwriter in Iowa is not greatly interested in what his counterpart in Norwich is doing. The company may have global reach, but the relevance of global management is muted, except for top management and selected high fliers.

In other companies, the need to integrate globally is far higher. Computer manufacturers and aerospace firms have highly integrated design, manufacturing and supply which cross the globe. This is where the limits of technology become clear. In many of these organisations there is huge frustration in working in global, virtual teams. There is plenty of research on how to organise global firms, there is very little knowledge about the practice of running a global team. The team can have the protocols, goals, roles and responsibilities and communications in place, and it still does not work. The challenge is about people and power. Teams are built on trust: video conferencing does not build trust. Trust takes time and personal contact: these are expensive activities. The frustration comes because power is uneven: decisions, promotions, resource allocation and priorities are not decided democratically.

For managers who are not at the power centre of the global team, this is hugely frustrating: they have to double guess what will happen; they find their priorities being arbitrarily changed and they feel out of the power loop. Few firms are able to transcend geography.

Japanese firms tend to have Japanese bosses and American firms tend to have American bosses. Howard Stringer and Carlos Ghosn (CEOs of Sony and Nissan respectively) and a few others are notable precisely because they are exceptional. This home country bias matters in a global world. It is easy, but possibly wrong, to suggest that companies should lose their home country bias and become truly supranational. In theory, this should help them win the war for talent: firms should be able to attract and promote the best talent regardless of nationality. Home country bias deters high-flying nationals from other countries: they do not want to be excluded from the magic circle of power.

The current reality is that most firms do not value diversity. Even where there is diversity of faith, gender and race firms still value conformity to a single set of values. This is celebrated in phrases such as "The one firm firm" (McKinsey) or "Blue Box Thinking" (American Express). There is good reason for this. Conformity aids understanding and improves ease, if not effectiveness, of decision making. Firms preach diversity but practice conformity. Cultural conformity is reflected in conformity around gender, race and nationality in the board room. When women get into the board room, it is usually to make tea and clean up. PwC and Monks estimated that in 2007 women represented 3.5% of main board executive directors among the top 350 publicly quoted companies in the UK.

Valuing conformity over diversity has its price. Part of the price is in the war for talent, as shown above. But it also raises the stakes in global competition. In the chapter on leadership we will see how different nationalities have fundamentally different views about what makes good leaders. Where countries are not competing against each other, this is a matter of anthropological interest only. Where countries are competing directly against each other, it starts to matter greatly. The result is not just a clash of economic models, but also of management models. The rise of Japan through the 1970s and 1980s was based on a different way of managing which the West simply did not understand until it was too late for several industries.

The power shift from the West to the rest of the world will not stop. To survive, firms need to learn new ways of organising (global teams, global talent) and new ways of competing. The problem is obvious, the solution is not. The solution will not be discovered by clever research: it will be discovered in the fog of war.

The rewards of power are becoming very unbalanced

This is not surprising. In a skills economy, skilled workers are cashing in and unskilled workers are dropping out. This can be seen in several ways.

First, life earnings are directly related to educational achieve-ment. The data is either very bleak or very encouraging, depending on which side of the skills divide you are. In earnings terms, someone with a professional, postgraduate qualification will earn three or four times as much as someone who dropped out of high school. The US Department of Labor data shows that each level of qualification increases earnings and decreases the likelihood of unemployment (2008).

Qualification	Unemployment rate (%)	Median weekly earnings ($)
Professional degree	1.7	1522
Masters degree	2.4	1228
Bachelors degree	2.8	978
Some college, no degree	5.1	645
High school graduate	5.7	591
Less than High school diploma	5.9	426

Perhaps it is no surprise that the wealth gap and the skills gap mirror each other. Perhaps it is more surprising to find that the gap between rich and poor is increasing. This gap is most easily measured by the Gini coefficient which is a measure of income disparity. Historically, increasing affluence has been associated with increasing opportunity for all. The medieval period had a few very wealthy barons and countless poor peasants; the Industrial Revolution saw a few very wealthy business barons and countless poor workers. As national wealth rises, such income disparity normally declines: an affluent middle class starts to emerge and even at the bottom of the pyramid grinding poverty reduces: in European countries active wealth distribution through tax has accelerated this process. France, Italy and Germany have Gini coefficients of around 0.3, which is quite low (implying fairly equal distribution of incomes). Countries with high inequality include emerging economies (Brazil, Mexico). China also has very high income inequality with a Gini coefficient of 0.45: unfettered capitalist practice has overwhelmed Communist political theory. Chinese save because they know there is no real social security to protect them when things go wrong. And finally the US has the same level of income inequality as China.

Over the last 30 years income inequality has been growing in the US. The Gini coefficient for the US has risen from 0.4 to 0.47 from 1980 to 2006. In the absence of European style redistribution, this disparity is likely to increase. Income inequality has plenty of social and political implications for people to debate. From a management perspective, this is clear evidence that mature economies are becoming skills economies: the skilled survive, the unskilled will struggle.

Conclusions

Most revolutions are dangerous because they happen too fast: there is no time to react and no way of knowing who will win and lose. The four power revolutions for management are dangerous because they are so slow. Like geological shifts which see the rise of mountains and the movement of continents, it is more or less impossible to see the changes from day to day. But the changes are unstoppable and are reshaping the world of management. The danger is that by the time we realise the changes are happening, it is too late for us to react. We find ourselves marooned on the wrong side of history.

Fortunately, revolutions create opportunities as well as dangers. There will be winners as well as losers. We can expect a period of upheaval and creative destruction in which old industries disappear and new industries emerge. If anyone had told the British in 1900 that they would lose nearly all of their coal, shipbuilding and apparel industries within 100 years, there would have been disbelief followed by fear: nothing short of cataclysm could lead to such loss. In practice, the loss of old industries creates space for new industries and new firms to emerge and for more wealth to be created. We cannot stop the revolution, but the brave can profit from it.

Chapter Four

Money: From CAPM to the Road to Ruin

In 1494 an Italian friar, Luca Pacioli, published a book on maths and algebra. Any book had to be pretty special to justify being printed just 50 years after Johannes Gutenberg developed the first printing press in Europe. Pacioli's book was special for two reasons. It was the first book on maths to be published in the vernacular as opposed to Latin or Greek: this made the mystery of maths accessible to a far wider audience. Second, the book contained a section which codified existing best practice among Venetian merchants for book keeping. Pacioli may not have invented accounting, but he was the first to summarise it in book form. Pacioli has defined standard practice for merchants and accountants ever since.

For 500 years Pacioli's systems of book keeping and accounting have survived remarkably well. A system created in the days of sailing ships and horse power has survived to the era of space ships and nuclear power. Not surprisingly, it is now showing signs of age.

Pacioli's system has run into trouble for two reasons.

First, the new world disorder is creating a series of fundamental technical flaws which seriously compromise traditional accounting.

Physical assets are decreasingly important as an indicator of a firm's value; equally, a firm's liabilities have changed sufficiently that the firm's balance sheet is increasingly unreliable without forensic examination of all the accounting notes. In management accounting, the increasing importance of indirect costs and overheads has made traditional functional accounting a misleading guide to the drivers of costs in a business. Many of these technical challenges are well known, but the solutions are less obvious. We are entering into the unknown: we need a modern day Pacioli to design a system for the next 500 years.

If the technical challenges are visible, they can at least be managed. Perhaps more dangerous is the second set of challenges facing traditional accounting systems. Accounting is not just about dry book keeping. It is increasingly about power, politics and purpose. In most firms the budget process is in theory a technical process of allocating resources efficiently to maximise returns. In practice it is a political process where managers seek to maximise resources and minimise their commitments: naïve managers accept "challenging" targets in a fit of machismo that they later regret. More adroit managers negotiate hard for a soft budget.

The challenges of accounting pale into insignificance compared to the problems of financial theory. CAPM, the capital asset pricing model, was always unsound in theory, although challenging it would inevitably lead to a "D" grade from a business school finance professor. It has proved to be ruinous in practice. Not all of the credit crunch is the fault of CAPM, but it played a key role in giving spurious academic respectability to the nonsense which banks touted as sophisticated rocket science.

We will explore the full extent of these political and technical challenges with accounting and finance in four sections:

1.   Financial accounting
2.   Management accounting
3.   Budget processes
4.   Rewards and measures

In some areas, solutions are emerging. In other areas we are struggling like medieval merchants who did not have the benefit of Pacioli and his new fangled ideas about book keeping.

Financial theory and the road to ruin

Finance is the land of the rocket scientist. These are brilliant people who devise brilliant mathematical models to optimise investment decisions and make large amounts of money. At least, that is the theory. The practice is rather different. Reality rarely conforms to the warped theoretical world of the rocket scientist. When reality intrudes, disaster ensues. LTCM (Long Term Capital Management) was the classic hedge fund rocket built by rocket scientists. Myron Scholes and Robert C. Merton were board members of LTCM and shared the 1997 Nobel Prize for economics. Next year LTCM collapsed losing $4.6 billion because they had not modelled a financial crisis in Russia. They were amateurs compared to the top bankers who managed to make their fortunes and then write off over $1 trillion in the credit crunch of 2008–2009.

Financial theory and financial practice are far apart. Most practicing managers cannot build clever financial models and cannot lose $1 trillion. When there is a mismatch between theory and practice, either the theory is wrong or the practice is wrong. The overwhelming evidence is that the theory is wrong. This matters, because financial theory is about making rational investment decisions, about maximising returns on our resources. If we do not know how to do this, we will be wasting resources and missing opportunities. So we need to pay attention to financial theory, understand what is wrong and see how it can improve.

There are three basic problems with current financial theory:

- The theory itself is flawed
- Theory and practice are mismatched
- Alternative approaches are better

Financial theory is flawed
Mention "Capital Asset Pricing Model" (CAPM) or "Black-Scholes option pricing theory" and many sane people will quickly go insane. This is a fair response to the arcane world of financial theory. If this is your reaction, move quickly onto the next section which shows how theory and practice are mismatched.

The Capital Asset Pricing Model (CAPM) is at the heart of financial theory. It is the method which determines the discount rate, or the rate of return, used to evaluate financial decisions. It is a critical equation. If CAPM determines a rate of return which is too low (say, 1%), we will invest in projects which destroy value. If CAPM determines a rate of return which is too high (say, 50%), then we will miss out on investing in some worthwhile projects.

CAPM is normally written as an equation:

$$COE = R_f + \beta(R_m)$$

Where:

COE is the cost of equity

R_f is the risk free rate, taken as the yield to redemption on a government bond

β is beta, the specific risk associated with a stock or a project

R_m is the risk premium on the market: the extra return required for investing in stocks, not safe government bonds.

This equation can give results ranging from a cost of equity between 4% and 40%. In practical terms, you may as well make a number up and stick with it. Let's see how you can come to such a diverse set of outcomes, using data from one day in April 2009.

- The risk free rate is somewhere between 0.86% and 3.02% using the yield to redemption on one-year and 10-year government bonds.
- Beta of individual stocks on the stock market is typically between about 0.7 and 1.5, depending on the volatility of the stock and whether you use a one-year or five-year calculation of beta. The beta for investing in an individual project is more art than science. A cost cutting programme may have a beta of 0.5 (if you lay people off, you know the financial impact even if you have no idea of the human impact); starting a new business may justify a beta of four. Risk is a matter of perception and negotiation.
- The historic risk premium on the market is somewhere between 5.6% and 8.9%.

If we use the low estimates above, we achieve a cost of equity of about 3.9% (0.86 + (0.5 * 5.6)). If we use the high estimates above, we achieve a cost of equity of 38.6% (3.02 + (4 * 8.9)) This is a ten fold difference in the required return: either you need to earn 3.9% or about 39%. The CAPM yields spurious accuracy for basic management judgements. Worse, it misleads managers. Because the beta on stocks is normally between 0.7 and 1.5, managers think the beta or risk of individual projects will be between 0.7 and 1.5. In practice, the spread of risk is much greater. Reducing costs through better supplier management or quality improvements has a beta close to zero; entering a new market has a beta as high as a venture capitalist dares to imagine. Wise managers will not look at a single point outcome: they will realise that each investment opportunity might lead to a range of outcomes with different levels of probability. However, the CAPM provides a single point solution which looks sophisticated, but fails to capture the diversity of possible outcomes. Once managers focus on the range of outcomes, the debate becomes more productive: it can start to focus on how to mitigate against the worst risks and increase the chances of the best outcome happening. It is better to rely on judgement than on a formula when making major investments.

The historic risk premium number is also a real problem: it works neither in theory nor in practice. The risk premium is normally calculated by estimating the excess return on stocks versus government bonds over a very long period of 100 years or more. There are a few obvious problems with this:

- Finance professors keep on saying that we cannot predict the future from the past: "The dice has no memory". And yet they estimate the risk premium precisely on the basis that the past does predict the future: make your minds up, guys.

- Estimates of the historic risk premium vary from 8.9% to 5.6%: estimates are significantly skewed by survivor bias. Estimates based on US and UK stock markets are one thing: many other stock markets have been wiped out completely by world wars, revolutions and national bankruptcy. Estimates of the risk premium are influenced as much by events from 1880 to 1900 as they are by events from 1990 to 2010. Academics believe that investment policy in the age of the space ship is shaped by the age of the steam ship.

- Estimates are deeply unhelpful over the short to medium term. The notion that stocks produce an excess return over bonds of 8.9% produces a hollow laugh in Japan where stocks peaked at nearly 40 000 in December 1989. 20 years later the Nikkei would have risen to about 220 000 based on excess returns of 8.9% a year and zero inflation. In reality, the index hit 7000 in 2009. It is a theory which can lead straight to poverty (see also LTCM above). Japanese investors have become less interested in return *on* capital and more interested in return *of* capital: that is an attitude the West is discovering in the credit crunch. US investors have discovered that equities have underperformed bonds from 1969 to 2009: believing in the risk premium has been a money losing belief for anyone who started saving in the last 40 years.

- Applying the historic risk premium to the value of the UK or US markets as a whole shows that the whole market was undervalued from 1970–1990: either the market was wrong or the theory was wrong. Reality is rarely wrong. The only way to match market reality to the risk premium is to use a forecast risk premium. A simplified version of the forecast risk premium is:

$$R_m = D_y + G - R_f$$

Where:

> R_m is the risk premium on the market,
> D_y is the dividend yield on the market,
> G is the long term nominal growth of dividends and
> R_f is the Risk Free rate of return.

There are variations on this model, which was developed in a paper by Owen and Wilson in 1988: doubts about the validity of CAPM and the risk premium are not simply a child of the credit crunch. The problems with the risk premium have long been known.

CAPM is flawed in theory and can be ruinous in practice. Managers need a better way of deciding what an acceptable rate of return should be. Financial theory is failing to do this in any meaningful way. It is a gap waiting to be filled by anyone who is not just smart, but practical as well. In the meantime, managers have a radical option at their disposal: rely on judgement not on dangerous formulas. Managers can make informed judgements about risks, likely returns and alternative investment opportunities. At any one time a firm consists of a portfolio of investment opportunities: you do not need CAPM to decide which opportunities are the most attractive. You need judgement.

Financial theory and practice are mismatched

Let us set aside the theory for a moment, and make an assumption that a firm requires a 10% return on capital. In theory it should proceed with projects which yield more than 10% return, and avoid projects which yield less than 10%. To simplify this further we will use 10% as a simple hurdle rate, and ignore NPV (net present value) and other important refinements.

Armed with this target, the firm proceeds to invest heavily in projects earning slightly above 10%. It should be a success. Instead, it goes bust. How did the theory turn out so spectacularly badly in practice? There are at least three reasons:

- *Game playing.* Once managers know that they need to promise a 10% return, they will construct their spreadsheets to promise a 10% return. They will start at the bottom right hand corner of the spreadsheet with the desired answer and then fix the assumptions in the rest of the spreadsheet to get the right answer. They then submit the spreadsheet and if the planning department fails to spot their dodgy assumptions, the managers win the lottery and get the investment wanted. The 10% is likely to be far too optimistic, but by the time that is discovered the manager will have moved on, collected a bonus or promotion and the original proposal will have long been forgotten.
- *Events.* Surprises are rarely positive: customers want to pay less, suppliers and staff want to be paid more, competitors match your every move, regulations and taxmen do not get less onerous and recessions happen. Even honest spreadsheets and projections rarely produce the returns expected.
- *The averages problem.* At any one time a firm will have a portfolio of projects. Some will be successes, some failures, some marginal projects and some projects in development and costing money. The successes need to be very profitable to pay for the failures and the development efforts. They need to yield not 10%, but 20% or 30% or more to pay for other projects. If a

firm targets an average return of 10%, individual projects need to be able to produce far more than 10%.

The problems of game playing, events and averages mean that it would be suicidal for any firm to accept projects promising a yield of 10–12% if the firm wants to achieve an average 10% return. The hurdle rate needs to be set much higher, and in practice it is. The theoretical required return is at best irrelevant, and at worst it is positively dangerous. In practice, successful firms all have profit sanctuaries where the returns are far in excess of the cost of capital. These are areas where the firm has an "unfair" advantage in so far as there is inadequate competition. For nearly 30 years Boeing had a wonderful profit sanctuary called the 747: there was no real competition to it. This profit sanctuary enabled it to invest in updating the rest of its civilian airline fleet. If a firm only targets the basic cost of capital, it will never reach it: there will be too many disappointments which water down the average return. In practice, managers need to ignore the theory: they need to maximise the returns wherever they can.

In practice, investment decisions are far more than a financial decision for a firm. When assessing an investment proposal strong managers will take three main factors into account:

1. The financial investment case. Experienced managers know that the number in the bottom right hand corner of the spread-sheet has been fixed to produce a desirable answer. The real value of the spreadsheet and investment case is not about the answer: it is about the assumptions which have been made to produce the spreadsheet. The financial investment case is less

about checking numbers and more about checking thinking and challenging assumptions. Good thinking is more important than numeracy in evaluating the financial case for a project.

2. The strategic case. Diversification should be a dirty word in business. Business history is littered with the wreckage of firms that decided to diversify away from the core business by chasing financially attractive opportunities elsewhere. Even dedicated conglomerates like ITT, TRW, Litton and Hanson have shone for a while and then imploded. Good investments fit with and support the rest of the firm's strategy. The strategic case is as important as the financial case for investment.

3. The quality of people making the proposal. An A grade proposal from a B team will always struggle. It will lack credibility: neither the numbers nor the delivery capability will be believed. The B grade proposal from the star A team is more likely to succeed: managers back people as much as they back ideas. The star team with a good track record is more likely to deliver than the B team. Managers with little track record will, if they are smart, enlist the support of A team stars to borrow their credibility and make the proposal fly.

Alternative approaches to financial theory

Financial theory is an alphabet soup of tools and theories: NPV, EVA, WACC, CAPM, IRR, DCF, COE and more all have their places. The proponents of EVA (economic value added) will wax lyrical about their approach and spit blood at anyone who uses something so naïve as NPV (net present value). Like medieval theologians debating how many angels can stand on a head of a pin, financial theory is full of clever people debating arcane irrelevance.

Most firms tend to use one of four simple approaches to making a financial evaluation of a project:

Payback period
Hurdle rate
Raising EPS (earnings per share)
NPV (net present value).

We will briefly explore the use and abuse of each of these.

Payback period is very simple: take the initial cost or investment required and see how many years it takes to pay back the original outlay. For instance, one firm uses a three-year payback period. If you fire someone, it may cost a year's salary, but you gain that back in a year. That is a one-year payback which easily beats the three-year goal. This has the virtue of simplicity, but it fails to recognise any benefits (cash flow) from the project which may come after the payback period. Payback can be misleading when assessing major investments, like an oil field or a new drug: the payback is very long ("Unattractive") even although the investment may in reality be highly attractive.

Hurdle rates have been discussed above: set a goal that each project must return at least, say 15%. Adjust the hurdle rate for the risk of the project. Risky projects should return more than less risky projects. Again, this is relatively simple although it raises the question of what the right hurdle rate should be. It runs into difficulty when there are too many projects of different sizes which beat the hurdle rate: with limited resources, firms need another way of optimising resource allocation.

Raising EPS (earnings per share) is a favourite of CEOs wanting to justify a takeover. This is normally no more than an accounting game. If a firm with a high PE ratio buys a firm with a low PE ratio, the EPS of the acquirer automatically rises. This looks great, except that no real value has been created and study after study shows that nearly all the gains of a takeover go to the shareholders of the acquired company: they pocket the 30–40% bid premium that the acquirer has had to pay for their firm. EPS games are a good way for CEOs to fool investors into thinking that the CEO is doing a good job.

NPV (net present value) takes in all of the cash flows associated with a project (initial investment, running costs and returns). It then discounts all those cash flows back into today's value using a hurdle rate (see above). This is probably the most rigorous form of assessing an investment, and the most complicated to produce. As a simple version, imagine that a credit card company acquires a new customer. Based on thousands of previous examples, the credit card company will be able to profile the expected cash flow from each sort of customer acquired from different sorts of channel. A simplified calculation might look like this:

Year	0	1	2	3	4	5
Acquisition cost $	500					
Net cash flow $	−500	150	150	150	150	150
Discount factor	1	0.87	0.76	0.66	0.57	0.50
Discounted cash flow $	−500	130	113	99	86	75

In this example we have assumed it costs $500 dollars to acquire the customer who produces net cash flow to the company each year of $150 for five years before defecting to another company which gives a better deal. The credit card company uses a discount rate of 15%. The net result is that this customer is marginally attractive, producing an NPV of just $3 over five years. From a management perspective, the real interest is not about the simple investment decision. The real interest comes when you use this as a management tool to raise profitability by asking some simple questions:

- How can we reduce the cost of acquisition – are there alternative channels (magazines, affinity groups, member get member programmes etc.) which are less expensive?
- How can we raise the net annual cash flow by cross-selling, reducing servicing costs or raising prices?
- How can we stop attrition and retain the loyalty (and cash flows) of this customer for longer?

NPV, like most financial theory, is of limited use by itself. The theory is not a substitute for judgement. When the theory is allied to insight and judgement, it can become a powerful management tool. It is, however, also dangerous. All NPV calculations are based on a discount rate, or cost of equity calculation. As we have seen above, financial theory has provided no sound way of determining a discount rate. Once again, managers have to rely on judgement, not on theory.

Financial theory beyond the private sector

Resource allocation is important and we need some way of knowing how to do it. Financial theory assumes a for-profit world where the goal is to maximise financial return on financial investment. Financial theory has nothing to offer the non profit and government world which accounts for 30–45% of GDP of advanced economies. This is a non trivial omission. It is worth a quick detour into this world to see how it copes without financial theory.

The overwhelming message is that the public sector is not good at using resources well. We will explore the reasons for this further in the section on rewards and measures. But the exceptions are instructive: they show the challenges and how resource allocation can be done well without financial theory.

To make the point, we will take one case: Teach First. Teach First is a not-for-profit which recruits outstanding graduates and turns them into exceptional teachers in the most challenging inner city schools in the UK. Within seven years of starting, it has become a top 10 graduate recruiter in the UK; up to 10% of Oxford and Cambridge graduates apply for the programme each year; market demand from schools and head teachers is very strong and it has a sustainable economic model. It is, therefore, reasonably successful. The board is asked to choose between the following sorts of investments:

- increasing recruiting capacity to attract a wider pool of great graduates;
- building a knowledge base of best teaching practices to raise performance;
- rebuilding the IT system to sustain the infrastructure of the organisation.

Financial theory offers us no way of making choices between any of these: we cannot assign an economic return or NPV to any of them. In the long term, there will be returns to society: better educated kids get better jobs and pay more tax, while kids who drop out of school may become drains on social security and the prison system. But we cannot capture those benefits neatly in a five-year NPV calculation for Teach First.

Despite this, Teach First has so far made smart investment decisions. It has typically had less than half the recruiting budget of top private sector firms, and has competed with them effectively. The secret of success is not hard to find. Teach First cannot use theory and cannot use financial goals: instead it has to use old-fashioned judgement and focus on its mission. As managers, we need to find the courage to back our judgement more and rely on theory less.

Financial theory: Conclusions

Financial theory and practice are seriously mismatched. Managers who follow financial theory to make investment decisions are likely to be led astray. Managers need to break free from financial ortho-doxy to make sound financial decisions. Effective managers already know this.

In practice, making sound investment decisions is based on the following:

- Set a high hurdle rate, a multiple of what theory would imply, so that the successful projects can make up for failures. Set different hurdle rates for different types of project: cost cutting programmes are more painful but less risky than ambitious new product proposals.
- Use a financial case as an opportunity to test assumptions and assess different scenarios. Recognise that the number in the bottom right hand corner of the spreadsheet will have been fudged.

- Invest to support the strategy and direction of the firm: a strong financial case is never enough by itself. It has to fit with the broader aims of the firm.
- Back good managers as readily as you back a good plan: the quality of the team will determine both the quality of the plan and the quality of delivery and outcome.
- Be deeply suspicious of purely "strategic" investments which have no financial case. You can be sure of spending the money and be reasonably sure of seeing no return. Major IT projects are typical culprits of the "strategic" pitch. Top executives who lack IT skills rarely feel able to fight back against such a pitch.

All of this looks suspiciously as if managers need to use judgement in making investment decisions. And that is correct. Financial theory can provide some useful tools to managers. But the tools are an aid to judgement, not a substitute for judgement. Orthodox financial theory is extremely dangerous unless used with extreme care. Instead of worrying about the alphabet soup, enjoy the freedom and responsibility of using judgement.

Financial accounting: the road to irrelevance

Financial accounts are meant to give a "true and fair" view of a firm's financial position. This is important for investors, tax authorities and for management. The concepts of "true and fair" and "financial accounting" are rapidly becoming strangers to one another. At worst, financial accounting is a battleground between rogues and regulators. The rogues are CEOs and CFOs (Chief Financial Officers) who want to present the most flattering portrait of their position. The regulators meanwhile devise ever more rules to prevent the most flagrant abuses of financial accounting. It appears that the rogues are winning.

The credit crunch provided some of the more spectacular failures of accounting. In 2008 RBS (Royal Bank of Scotland) proudly announced profits of £10.2 billion. In 2009, these profits had suddenly become losses of £40.7 billion, equivalent to £8000 for every inhabitant of Scotland. These heroic losses did not appear out of nowhere: most of the losses came as a result of unwise lending in the sub-prime market in previous years. The toxic assets were there, but the accounts never picked them up. As a tribute to the flexibility of accounting, RBS announced it had actually made a profit of £80 million at the same time as declaring a £40.7 billion loss. The profit figure was defined as "underlying profit". This is about as reliable as the profits declared by start ups in the dot.com boom, where profits were defined broadly as sales before costs. The £40.7 billion loss was stated as loss before tax. Pick whichever version of reality you wish.

Clearly, the credit crunch was a special case. And banks are generally special cases, with accounts which bear little resemblance to the accounts of non financial organisations. But accounting is struggling to keep up with the new reality in all organisations. The heart of the problem is the changing nature of the balance sheet: once that changes, it can also have dramatic impacts on the P&L (profit and loss) statement.

In Pacioli's time, the balance sheet was relatively straightforward. Assets tended to be physical assets: stocks, cash, work in progress and perhaps a horse or some machinery. All these things can be valued relatively easily, and can be sold if necessary. Liabilities were equally clear. They were mainly a mix of debts to banks and suppliers and hopefully some retained profits for the owners.

The world has changed, and the balance sheet is no longer straightforward. Accounting value and economic value have become separated, as the simplified chart below shows:

	1500: Pacioli's world	2010
Assets	Cash	Brands
	Stocks	Human talent
	Work in progress	Patents, licences
	Machinery	Market presence
Liabilities	Shareholders' equity, retained earnings	Off balance sheet liabilities
	Debt to banks	Long-term contracts
	Debt to suppliers	Pensions

The assets of a firm are increasingly intangible. Accounting value and economic value have become separate concepts. The economic value of a firm like Microsoft, Google or a drug company will not be the sum of its offices, computers and some manufacturing (if that has not been outsourced). The economic value of these firms lies in their patents, their human talent and the intangible benefits of brand names, established market presence and customer relationships. A good firm has always been able to create economic value that exceeds the simple sum of its accounting assets. Historically, the market price of the S&P 500 compared to the accounting book value of its components has been just under 2: firms have been judged to be worth twice the value of the book value (book value being taken as shareholders' equity and retained earnings). By 2008, the price to book (or market value to book value) of the S&P 500 had risen to over 5. For high tech firms like Microsoft or Google, price to book ratios of 50 or more were common.

Perhaps more damaging is the liabilities side of the balance sheet, where once again a 500-year-old system is struggling to keep up with modern reality. The changing nature of modern liabilities raises two basic problems:

- Valuing the liabilities of the firm has become increasingly hard. Pensions liabilities are a swamp which can consume firms. GM has to earn $1400 from every car to pay the pensions and health care costs of its retirees. It is, effectively, a social security scheme supported by car making. British Airways in its 2008 annual report had shareholders' equity of £3 billion. No mention was made of its pension liabilities of £13.5 billion. The legacy of defined benefit schemes leaves companies with a huge obligation which varies dramatically on minor shifts in interest rates. UK pension regulation puts retirees' interests first, which creates huge tension with shareholders and existing workers.

- Some of the most important liabilities of the firm rest outside the accounting system. For instance, retailers normally enter into long term lease agreements. This makes sense until recession hits: then investors discover that retailers are highly geared plays on the economy. Similarly, many airlines choose to lease aircraft. If they borrowed money to buy the aircraft, the liability would be visible. An operational lease still creates the economic liability, but is not an accounting debt. High fixed costs are fine when times are good, but a disaster when times turn tough.

- In theory, all of this can be solved by more rules and more disclosure. This is the road that regulators are taking. A typical 10-K SEC filing (annual report) will now run to 200 pages. Most people do not have the time or energy to wade through such verbiage. Stock analysts are paid to do so, and do an abysmal job of it. In 2008, according to Bloomberg, a grand total of 6.7% of analysts' forecasts matched earnings outcomes for S&P 500 companies, despite the copious guidance given to them by Chief Financial Officers. Analysts are consistently over-optimistic, partly because they have to puff up the business of their employer. Infamously, Henry Blodget was voted No 1 internet analyst in 2000: in 2002 he made a $4 million settlement with the New York Attorney General when it was found that his emails to colleagues within Merrill Lynch conflicted with the views he had published. More disclosure is of little help if analysts are not truly independent.

The only people who dare to take an independent view of a business are the short sellers: they sniff out corporate accounting nonsense and put their own money where their mouth is when they find the nonsense. Inevitably, in the credit crunch the regulators on both sides of the Atlantic chose to stop short selling: if in doubt, shoot the messenger. Short sellers were not the problem: they were part of the solution because they looked past accounting value to find the economic value and prospects of the firm. They established the truth which accounts successfully hide.

We do not suffer a lack of accounting detail: we suffer a lack of judgement and focus. Investors do not need yet more disclosure: the bigger the haystack, the harder it is to find the needle. We need accountants and managers who have the courage to produce a "true and fair" view. That would require a short statement which looks both back at results achieved and forwards to what might be achieved and the risks involved. Managers have to live up to budget commitments within a firm: perhaps top managers should start making budget commitments to their shareholders.

If accounts are unreliable in giving shareholders a "true and fair" view of the business, then they are far down the road to irrelevance.

Management accounting

Management accounting, like financial accounting, is struggling to keep up with a changing world. In Pacioli's time, merchants had to make do without consultants, IT help desks, Strategic Human Capital Divisions, computers, mobile phones and cappuccino machines. They lived in a world without all of the corporate life support systems which both enable and imprison the modern manager. The rise in corporate services means more overheads and an explosion of indirect costs.

To understand how the rise of indirect costs is affecting accounting, take the example of a baker. Two hundred years ago the village baker had pretty simple accounts. He sold bread and paid for flour, fuel and wages before making some profit. The more bread he sold, the more flour and fuel he used. The cost of each loaf of bread was easy to calculate. Now imagine a modern, industrial scale bakery. Flour and fuel might be only 10–20% of the bakery's costs. The rest of the costs will go on capital depreciation and interest payments on the plant and equipment; on buying and maintaining IT systems; on advertising and corporate overheads. To make matters more complicated, it may produce 100 different sorts of bakery product, in different volumes and with differing ease of baking. It is now very hard to know exactly how much each bakery item cost to produce. Someone, somewhere, is going to have to allocate a huge amount of costs across the 100 different product lines, and there is no easy way of doing so. The rise of indirect costs is making it harder to understand where profitability lies and what is driving costs. If we do not know which products are profitable and what is driving our costs, we are unlikely to be able to manage our business successfully.

To illustrate the point, we will take a highly simplified example of a widget maker who makes equal amounts of three sorts of widget: high price widgets (A), medium price widgets (B) and low price widgets (C).

Table 4.1 shows that all the widgets make a gross profit and make a contribution to overheads, which are roughly one third of revenues. So far, so good.

Table 4.1 Profitability before allocation of overheads

	A	**B**	**C**	**Total**
Volume	100	100	100	300
Unit price	15	12	8	
Total revenue	1500	1200	800	3500
Direct cost/unit	8	6	4	
Total cost	800	600	400	1800
Gross profit	700	600	400	1700
Overhead				1200
Net profit				500

Being a traditional company, the widget maker allocates overheads to each product on the basis of volume. Because equal amounts of each product are sold, each product bears equal amounts of overheads. This is a simple and normal way of allocating overheads in many functionally organised companies. The result shows that the cheap widgets only just break even. Perhaps the company should ditch the product line, or try to raise prices of the cheap widgets. See Table 4.2.

Table 4.2 Overhead allocated by unit volume

	A	B	C	Total
Gross profit	700	600	400	1700
Overhead	400	400	400	1200
Net profit	300	200	0	500

At this point, the manufacturing director points out that the cheap widgets are cheap because they do not require much effort, whereas the expensive one requires great effort. The cheap widgets are produced to one spec in one run with no machine changeovers and no machine downtime. The expensive widgets are more or less custom made and require huge amounts of downtime as machines are changed over repeatedly. So the finance director decides to adjust his calculations (Table 4.3) and allocate overheads in proportion to revenues. Suddenly, the cheap widgets appear profitable and the much neglected standard line of B widgets appears to be the most profitable line.

Table 4.3 Overhead allocated in proportion to revenue

	A	B	C	Total
Gross profit	700	600	400	1700
Overhead	514	411	274	1200
Net profit	186	189	126	500

The manufacturing director suspects this does not go far enough. He works with the sales manager and logs all activity for each product. They discover that 60% of indirect time and costs are expended on the expensive A line: not just machine downtime, but invoicing small batches for many different customers, scheduling challenges, dealing with customer enquiries and selling effort all make the A line very costly to serve. The cheap C line, which is just produced for one big customer, is very cheap to produce and sell. The results in Table 4.4 show that the C line is now the most profitable and the A line is making a loss.

Table 4.4 Overhead allocated by activity (work expended)

	A	B	C	Total
Gross profit	700	600	400	1700
% of overhead	60	30	10	
Overhead	720	360	120	1200
Net profit	−20	240	280	500

Depending on how the widget maker does his cost allocation, either A, B or C lines are the most profitable. The C line may be losing money or making money and the A line may be losing money or making money. If you have the wrong information, you are going to make the wrong decisions. Allocating costs is important and increasingly difficult.

Cost allocation and the widget maker's dilemma
In theory, ABC (activity based costing) provides an elegant solution to these problems. ABC was popularised in the Harvard Business Review in an article by Cooper and Kaplan in 1988. The timing was fortuitous. A few years later Hammer and Champy published *Reengineering the Corporation* which turned out to be the

must-have consulting and cost cutting fad of the 1990s. Re-engineering and ABC are soul mates: they both turn the organis-ation on its side. Instead of looking at functional silos, they look at processes and how they work across the silos of the organisation. It is no coincidence that ABC also had its heyday in the 1990s. Since then, re-engineering has gone into decline: it has become little more than cost cutting with a smile, where the smile is an optional extra. ABC has declined with re-engineering. In good times, cost discipline and process efficiency seem less important: the credit crunch may offer a temporary reprieve for both approaches.

We have neither the time nor the space here to show how ABC works, which hints at why it has gone into decline. It is a very powerful tool for understanding and managing costs, but it is also a very demanding tool. It soaks up considerable management time, normally needs outside expert help which makes it expensive, and is best done as a special analysis once every few years. Attempts to integrate ABC into enterprise software have been largely shunned: it is less of a normal accounting tool and more of a special analysis tool.

In practice, most management accounting remains true to the principles laid out by Pacioli over 500 years ago. Managers focus on functional costs: this can be misleading (see the widget case) but it is simple and it maintains a high degree of management account-ability. If a departmental budget is missed, the departmental head is to blame: accountability for ABC costs is less clear.

As ever, practice outruns theory. Functional costs may be misleading and ABC may be too complicated. But that does not stop managers creating simple, practical measures which they use to drive performance. Different industries tend to focus on their own unique measures of productivity and profitability, for instance:

- Credit card companies: NPV (net present value) per customer
- Airlines: utilisation and revenue per available kilometre
- Hotels: average revenue per room night
- Professional services: utilisation
- Banking: cost/income ratio
- Retailers: sales per square foot/metre and growth in like for like (same store) sales

Clearly, these are not the only measures each industry uses. But in each case they are reasonably strong measures of whether the business is going in the right direction or not.

Management accounting is caught between two stools. On one side it is clear that traditional management accounting tools are becoming increasingly unreliable for businesses which have large amounts of indirect overhead to allocate. On the other side, there is no satisfactory replacement. The experience of ABC shows that management accounting is likely to progress faster than financial accounting. Management accounting is free to experiment without the dead hand of the regulator, and the management have a pressing need to have good information on which to base decisions. As with much of the management revolution, management accounting is work in progress.

The budget process

Budgets are about allocating scarce resource effectively. It should be a rational process designed to optimise the resources and returns of the firm. Anyone who has lived through a budget process knows that it is not rational. It is a deeply political process in which managers scramble for as much resource, in return for the minimum commitments, as possible. The equation for top management is reversed: they are seeking the maximum return for the minimum resource. So the budget process is a three way battle between top management (supported by their planning department) and middle management, and between different groups of middle managers who are all competing for the same small pot of company resource.

The budget process exposes two unlikely truths about organisations:

- The real competition for most managers is not in the marketplace. The real competition is sitting at a desk nearby. Market competition may steal market share, but unlike your colleagues they will not steal your budget pool, bonus or promotion. Internal competition is far more severe than external (market) competition in most organisations.
- Organisations are set up for conflict. Conventional theory is that organisations are cooperative bodies. They are not. Each department, business, product group and geography has differing priorities and competing claims on the organisation. It is through the process of internal conflict and competition that the best ideas are slowly sifted out: sometimes it is not the best ideas but the best political operators who win. Internal competition can be brutal.

The rules of engagement for budget warfare are never written down but are normally well understood by all the players:

- Appear objective and focused on corporate goals. In practice, managers use data like drunks use lamp posts: for support, not illumination. Managers are not looking for the truth. They are seeking the best budget settlement possible, and will use data selectively to support their point.
- Get your retaliation in first. Strike early and frame the debate around your expectations: talk to senior management before the formal process starts. Keep the dialogue going to reinforce your position. Such base politics now has academic credibility. Daniel Kahneman, who won the Nobel Prize for economics in 2002, noted in his work on decision making that anchoring (framing) and repetition are two key influences on how people make decisions. In other words, decisions are not purely rational.
- Do not over deliver on this year's budget. Success this year simply means higher expectations for next year. If this year is going well, sandbag: delay as much of the good news into next year which then starts well. In the public sector, this takes the form of departments desperately spending taxpayers' cash as year end nears so that they do not have their budget cut next year. The political reality is that maintaining departmental resources is more important than looking after the taxpayer's money.

In theory, a Darwinian budget process need not be bad. Competition and survival of the fittest may find the best allocation of company resources. We should not complain if the budget process is political, vicious, unpleasant and hard work. Managers are paid to live with that sort of nonsense. We should only complain if the budget process results in poor allocation of scarce resources. In this respect, there is a minor and a major problem with most company budgeting processes.

The minor problem with most budgeting is that it takes time and effort: it is an overhead distraction from more value adding activities. And the game playing risks letting political managers win soft budget settlements which benefit them personally, but damage the organisation as a whole. This is a minor problem because it is well known. Most senior managers have played the budget game successfully as middle managers: they know all the tricks and are normally able to limit the damage done by such game playing.

The major problem is that the budget process is based on incremental thinking. The best predictor of next year's budget is this year's budget, plus or minus a bit for inflation and performance. Incremental thinking makes managers prisoners of the past: we take what we have inherited and carry on as before, perhaps running a little harder to keep up with the competition who are also running harder. But we cannot keep running harder for each year without eventually collapsing. At some point we have to start acting smarter: find a different route, buy a bicycle or trip up the competition. Most company budgets are not about acting smarter: they are about sweating harder.

When the budget and planning process becomes a substitute for strategic thinking, then the organisation is condemned to running harder, not smarter. Strategic thinking often cuts across departments and takes more than a year to implement. In other words, the one year, departmental budget prevents any sort of strategic thinking or action. Thinking within the budget box will not help on basic challenges such as:

- redefining the company portfolio of activities: selling and acquiring businesses;

- growing new internal capabilities, building new products and markets;
- redesigning work, re-engineering and overhauling the organisation.

In practice, most firms spend far too long on the budget process and far too little on the strategic process. The budget process is a safe process: the rules of engagement are known to all and the risks from getting it wrong are low. The strategic process is not safe for management: most lack experience of it, do not know the rules of engagement and the price of getting it wrong is very high. While the budget process is very methodical, the strategic process tends to be highly opportunistic or crisis driven: at best, it consists of an occasional report from consultants to senior management which is then communicated in garbled form to other managers. The result is a vast hole in the centre of most budgets: they are driven without true strategic direction or understanding.

In theory, budgets should be more strategic. But as long as strategic thinking is outsourced to consultants, that is not going to happen. Smart budgeting does not sort successful from unsuccessful organisations. Ford and GM have had very sophisticated planning departments and budget processes, and yet they have had their lunch stolen by Honda and Toyota. None of the successful (or unsuccessful) dot.com businesses have been made or broken by the quality of their budget process. They have succeeded or failed depending on the quality of their business model and delivery.

Clearer strategic thinking will minimise the problems of politics and incremental thinking. But given that budgeting is low risk and strategy is high risk, we can expect political budgets and incremental thinking to dominate for a long time yet in legacy organisations.

New organisations, unencumbered by history, are the ones that have the luxury of acting strategically rather than becoming prisoners of the past through the budget process.

Conclusions

Finance theory and accounting are deeply flawed. Apologists for them will argue that, like democracy, they are the worst methods except for all the alternatives. If the alternatives are simple formulas and rules, then the apologists are right: there are no better formulas or rules. The management challenge is to know how to deal with such imperfection.

The main conclusion is not to rely on formulas and rules: instead, rely on judgement. When formulas become a substitute for thinking, disaster ensues. In the case of the credit crunch, the disaster is going to cost us $4 trillion, according to the IMF. That is enough to cover the entire planet in $100 bills: that would probably have been a better use of the money than wasting it on banks and bankers. Poor accounting, unthinking reliance on CAPM and poor attitudes to risk all contributed to the $4 trillion loss.

The critical shift in thinking is to understand that neither financial theory nor accounting give reliable answers to management challenges. Used wisely, they can provide a platform for further thinking, for testing assumptions and exploring alternatives. In other words, they are not an end point, they are a starting point. We will grow old and die before effective financial theory or accounting is introduced. We cannot and need not wait for perfection. The challenge is to using the existing, imperfect, tools to ask the right questions and discover the right answers.

Chapter Five

Information: From Deficit to Hyperinflation

For the last 30 years, IT has been transforming the business landscape. It is neither the first, nor last, technological marvel to change the nature of industry. Arguably the advent of the railways brought about as much change by enabling the first Industrial Revolution to happen. Others will argue for the advent of the internal combustion engine, flight, electricity or telephones as the greatest transformative technology of business history. In future, there will be other technologies which dazzle our successors and convince them that they are living in a time of unprecedented technological change.

Instead of arguing over which technology has brought about the greatest change, perhaps we should instead accept that transformative technology is the normal condition in which firms work. Even the nature of the IT revolution has consistently changed over the last 30 years: from mainframes to desk tops to cloud computing; from landlines and faxes to mobile phones and email and Blackberries; from stand alone computers to the internet which itself has gone through several generations of evolution.

Predicting what technology will evolve or how it will be exploited is pointless. What we take for granted today was simply not seen yesterday: successes are discovered in the market rather than predicted in books. Google's paid search is now the obvious way to monetise search: others tried subscriptions (AOL) or banner advertising (Yahoo!). Facebook and Twitter have succeeded on the web: Boo.com (clothes retailing) and Webvan (groceries) failed. After the event we can be very wise. If we were wise and courageous before the event we would be very rich.

We may not be able to predict the future of technology, but we must learn how to manage it. The evidence so far seems to be that the technology has become more sophisticated than the humans. We have not learned how to handle either the technology or its application in management life. We are in a middle of a technology revolution, and we do not know where it will take us. We are being led by it, rather than leading it. We hope that technology will lead us to a prosperous and sustainable future; we fear it may be like Frankenstein's monster: our creation which we can no longer control.

The two basic challenges for managers are:

- How to manage technology effectively
- How to manage the application of technology to business.

How to manage technology effectively

Global spending on technology is huge. IDC estimates that in 2010 business and government will spend $1.5 trillion on technology. That will be split as follows:

- Software: $327 billion
- Hardware: $562 billion
- IT services: $587 billion

The Gartner group came up with a similar estimate for 2009, but added in another $1.9 trillion for telecommunications. To put these numbers in perspective, the entire GDP of the UK was just $2.1 trillion in 2009. Technology is also becoming a very large employer. IBM and Accenture alone employ 571 000 worldwide, compared to Ford and GM who employ just 495 000. The gap is growing fast. The new is replacing the old. The auto industry will point out that they have a hinterland of suppliers who depend on them; the IT industry will point out that every major business globally depends on them.

Given the scale of spending, it is important that management get good value for their money on technology. This is where it becomes reasonably clear that technology is more in control of management rather than the other way around. Typically, top managers in the executive suite are unable to quiz the IT director effectively: the IT director is able to run a fiefdom which others cannot challenge. Major systems upgrades are pushed through on the basis that they are strategic: if there is a business case it is often created after the event or ignored completely. In contrast, executives are very happy to comment on and criticise advertising: they think that since they have seen advertising as consumers, they must be experts at it. This is the fallacy that sports fans fall into: just because you watch something does not make you able to do it well. Although advertising gets plenty of scrutiny, at $450 billion annual spend, it is only one third the size of the IT industry. Executives review what is familiar, not what is important.

IT is the classic fear based sale: if you do not buy it, your firm is at risk of falling over. Few executives are ready to take that risk, or have the capability of assessing the risk. IT consultants and vendors are more likely to support the IT director, who is their source of future revenues, than give management an impartial or even critical view of the investment requirements of IT.

The data available supports the view that technology investment is widely wasted. The most widely quoted authority is the Standish report, which has regularly surveyed user executives since 1994. Their findings are:

- 31% of IT projects were cancelled before completion.
- 53% of projects were "challenged": they cost an average of 189% of budget, took 222% of the time budget and achieved 61% of the original specifications.
- 16% came in on time and on budget.

This is enormous waste, and inevitably the findings are controversial. In 2007 Sauer *et al.* decided to ask IT project managers, not users, to rate the performance of IT projects. Perhaps not surprisingly, IT managers rated themselves somewhat better. The Sauer survey gave the following results on the fate of IT projects:

- 9% abandoned
- 5% budget challenged
- 18% schedule challenged
- 59% good
- 7% stars which beat expectations

Because IT projects are internal firm initiatives, it is hard to gain an objective assessment of how well IT is or is not managed.

Firms are proud to report their successes, while they quietly bury their IT failures from public view. On the one occasion when all firms had to take on an IT project in public, the results were illuminating. The great Y2K ("Year 2000") project was required to make sure that all computers were ready for the new millennium. It is a story which gives a glimpse into the challenges of managing IT.

The Y2K problem started in the early days of computing, in an era of very limited processing power or memory. To save space, the year would be written as 72 or 68 instead of 1972 or 1968. Alan Greenspan (Chairman of the Federal Reserve 1987–2006) started his career writing code and recalled the reasoning for this:

> We started to write our programs so that they could be very clearly delimited with respect to space and the use of capacity. It never entered our minds that those programs would have lasted for more than a few years. As a consequence, they are very poorly documented. If I were to go back and look at some of the programs I wrote 30 years ago, I would have one terribly difficult time working my way through step-by-step.

In fairness: no-one expected such programmes to last so long, and no-one foresaw what huge problems would result from this minor piece of economising. Once people realised that computers would recognise year 2000 as year 00, all sorts of nightmarish outcomes were predicted. Utility companies would cease to work; nuclear power stations would malfunction, planes would fall out of the sky, the stockmarket would crash and you would get a $91 000 late fee for your DVD rental which the computer will have calculated is now 99 years overdue.

It might seem that spotting a date written as "99" and correcting it to "1999" would be a trivial task. In IT, nothing is trivial. For many firms, the first task was to work out what systems they actually used. In one bank over 600 different systems were used. Discovering them was like a major archaeological dig through the history of IT. Even the IT department did not know about the existence of many of them. And, as Greenspan indicated, there were no manuals and no documentation about many of the systems. No-one knew how they worked or how they might not work in the year 2000.

The cost of checking and changing all the relevant computer systems at AT&T alone came to $900 million. The business case for spending this fortune was very simple: you will gain no extra revenue, save no costs, improve no service and nothing will get better. But you will stay in business. Y2K was a highly unattractive but completely irresistible business case, as many IT business cases are. Globally, the cost of preparing for Y2K is estimated, by Gartner Group, to have been $1 trillion. The total return on that investment was zero.

No-one knows for sure what would have happened if the trillion dollars had not been spent on Y2K: the fact that the year 2000 passed off with only minor glitches can be used to prove that the preparation was either very good or that it was totally unnecessary. However, Italy gives us a clue to the answer. In November 1999 the Associated Press reported that "Italy is among the worst prepared countries in the West". They had not even set up a government panel to look into the problem until spring 1999. Their plan appeared to be to hope for a Papal miracle. They did little and spent less by way of preparation. When the clocks turned to start the year 2000, Italy did not implode. The only hangover they suffered was from the traditional New Year celebrations. Of the $1 trillion spent on Y2K, perhaps $900 billion was wasted, if the experience of Italy is anything to go by. The Y2K experience echoes the private experience of many firms:

- IT investment often has a poor business case, or no business case.
- No-one is sure if the spending was necessary or not, even after the event.
- Even trivial changes seem to be extremely expensive.
- Managers dare not oppose IT investment which they do not understand.
- Firms have acquired a vast legacy of systems and applications which they do not understand, which are poorly documented and which make any further changes extremely difficult to incorporate.

Management may not be fully in control of IT, but there are things which managers can do to reduce the pain. IT consultants recognise that there are some simple ways in which clients can assure themselves of disaster:

- Have an unclear goal or business need with no business case.
- Change requirements regularly during the programme.
- Change the governance and direction of the programme.
- Be slow in making any decision.

Sauer's IT survey broadly confirms these findings and then adds that the larger and longer a project is designed to be, the more likely it is to underperform. Every single project which took more than 200 man years to complete underperformed. Given these findings, it is no surprise that government regularly finds itself embroiled in IT fiascos: unlike private companies, government is unable to keep such fiascos out of public view.

The challenge of IT is exacerbated by the gulf between IT and the business. IT people and business people may speak the same language, but they find it very hard to understand each other. Masters of the business universe can turn into rages of anger or quivering wrecks of despair when asked to fix an IT problem at their home. Measuring the effectiveness of the IT department is very hard. Much of it comes down to a simple question: "Do I trust and respect the Chief Technology Officer?" Appearances can be as important as performance.

The IT monster may not be entirely under control, but it is hugely important. The beast will never be tamed completely, but managers can do more to help tame the beast. For a start, managers need to become more IT literate: go on courses and read the press. Spend more time talking to the IT staff, especially when there is not a crisis. Managers do not need to know the answers: they need to know the questions. If they can ask the right questions at the right time, they can make progress. And if we take the problems identified by Sauer and turn them around, we can do some simple things to make IT projects avoid meltdown:

- Make business drive the technology, not vice versa: be clear about the business needs and business goals first.
- Take time to understand and agree the requirements, then stick to them. Avoid changes.

- Do not change governance: maintain accountability by keeping the same team in charge throughout.
- Make decisions promptly.
- Keep projects down to a manageable size: if necessary, split a large programme into bite sized chunks.

Nothing can guarantee success, but we can reduce the risk of failure.

How to manage the application of technology to business

Humanity has always struggled with information and communications. For centuries, people had to cope with a deficit of information and communication. For the first time, we are having to deal with an excess of information and communication. We are only starting to learn how to deal with this excess. In many cases, dealing with excess is as difficult as dealing with a deficit of information and technology.

To understand the scale of the information revolution we will pay a quick visit to our ancestors to see how they coped before the revolution struck. Before the advent of the printing press, books were a rare and valuable commodity. A monk could take a lifetime to produce one copy of the Bible. Each word was precious. Going further back, Hammurabi issued the first law code to be written down and survive. The laws were literally written in stone and could be viewed by all. There were 282 laws which included everything from the cost of hiring a ship to getting your money back if you bought a defective slave. Such simplicity is long gone. In 1999 Tolley's guide to UK tax, ran to 4336 pages of indigestible, turgid legalese. It doubled to over 10 134 pages by 2008, and there are still no jokes in it. We are deep into the age of information overload.

A world with a deficit of information was also a world with a deficit of knowledge. For thousands of years, religion and superstition took the place of scientific enquiry. When Galileo suggested that the world might not be at the centre of the Universe, the church obliged him to recant his views on pain of torture and excommunication. Superstition and religion filled in knowledge gaps. Faith took the place of understanding. Little information and little knowledge went hand in hand with little progress. Trades were organised into guilds where knowledge was passed down from master to apprentice. The purpose of the system was to preserve and pass on knowledge, not to advance it.

There was some good news about the information deficit world. It meant that communication was valued. To this day, the Bambara, the main farming tribe in Mali, believe that "words are like gods. With words you can create whole new worlds in people's minds. Words can make people do anything. So treat words with respect. A wise person speaks little but means much." The contrast with today is stark. We are overloaded with information and it is ever harder to sort the meaning from the noise of daily communication.

In the world of information overload, we are having to rethink our assumptions about information and communication. More is no longer unquestionably better. The main challenge is managing the quality versus quantity of information and communication.

If we can do these things well, technology will be a wonderful servant to business. Manage it poorly and we will let technology become our master: it will shackle us 24/7 to the world of work. There will be little or no escape from the stress of deadlines, commitments and the need to answer the latest urgent email from colleagues in another time zone.

Because technology allows us to do more, we think we ought to do more. This assumption is a disaster which leads to all the modern malaise of being on call 24/7, enjoying constant stress. The examples are well known but bear repeating.

PowerPoint peril. In days long gone, a presentation was a big deal. If a graph or illustration was required, a graphic designer would be hired for the job. The time and cost was great so each slide was carefully thought through and the presentation would be short. Now it is possible to produce 200 slide presentations with snazzy graphics and visual effects. This leads straight to the world of death by PowerPoint. Good presentations can be judged by their length: shorter is better. Presentations are not complete when no more can be said: they are complete only when no less can be said. Brevity is very hard to achieve, but it forces focus on the key message and the story which needs to be told. That means that a good presentation is like a diamond: it benefits from good cutting.

Email hell has three versions: email overload, email stress and email wars.

- Email overload is not just a matter of spam offering drugs, weight loss, dodgy watches and a virus for your computer. Much worse is the legitimate corporate spam. Traditional snail mail was slow and expensive. Each letter meant something for both sender and recipient. There are no such costs to sending email. Emails are sent for trivia and copied not because we need them, but because we might need them. We might receive 100 emails a day: perhaps five to 10 of them are substantive and require proper attention. Because we can copy people on emails we do. Communication used to be on a need-to-know basis. Now it is based on a just-in-case basis, or more specifically a cover-your-back basis. The result is that effort is not saved by email, it is increased as everyone indulges in sending messages and replying to them just in case they need to cover their backs.

- Email stress comes from being shackled 24/7 to the demands of work by the electronic ball and chain of mobile phone and email. There is no escape. Trains and planes used to provide some respite until the invasion of the Blackberry. Because we can be on call all the time, we fear being out of touch, even on holiday. In truth, all managers are dispensable. Perhaps for that reason we fear being out of touch so we wear our electronic ball and chain with pride, and will even compare and compete with other executives to see who has the most modern and effective work shackles. Before email and mobile phone, managers had to learn the fine art of delegating, arranging cover and preparing for vacation. It worked. The world did not fall down when a manager was away for a while.

- Email wars start when we stop talking. It is commonplace to go into an office and find that people who can see each other across the room are emailing each other. They then find that misunderstandings occur. To avoid misunderstanding and protect their backs, they spell things out in detail in more emails which only serve to irritate the recipient. Email war breaks out. A 50-second conversation, which is very old fashioned, would have built the trust and understanding which emails cannot do.

Because we can send an email, and it takes a few seconds less than walking across the office, we do.

Conclusions

The search for more, better and timely information has been constant throughout the history of modern management. Managers have now been cursed by having their wishes fulfilled. We have gone from a drought of information to a flood of information. We are drowning in a non stop barrage of data. Technology hurts as much as it helps. It raises productivity, but it also raises expectations. The gains from technology do not accrue to managers: they accrue to more productive firms and better served customers.

Managers feel obliged to use technology to its full extent, because we can. Just because we can do something does not mean we should do it. We can drive cars at 200 kilometres an hour: that does not mean we should. We can buy vast amounts on credit cards, but perhaps we should not. We can use technology to its full potential, but perhaps we need to know how to use it better. Making the most of technology means using it less, not more. Technology has to be the servant, not the master, of our intentions. We have learned how to create brilliant technology, but we have not learned how to control it: the beast is out of control.

For 200 years, technology has been transforming society and work. Wave after wave of innovation has changed lives and changed the way we work. The pace of innovation is unlikely to slow down. The challenge for managers is to keep pace with a never ending technological revolution.

Chapter Six

Knowledge: From Ignorance to the Disintegration of the Firm

Knowledge presents us with a paradox: compared to our ancestors we are collectively smarter but individually more ignorant, relative to the sum of human knowledge. Firms both benefit and suffer from this paradox. Perhaps we first need to understand the paradox, and then understand how firms deal with it.

The sum of human knowledge is perhaps doubling every 20 years. As with information, we have emerged from an era of knowledge deficit to knowledge surplus: there is simply too much knowledge for any person to understand personally. Our ancestors relied on superstition to fill in any knowledge gaps. We rely on experts, or Google, to do the same. To illustrate the difference, compare how we live to a medieval peasant. The peasant could make more or less everything required for daily life: if something went wrong he or she could repair it to an acceptable degree. We have much more than the peasant. We have no idea how to make the most of our daily goods, from cars to mobile phones to the plastic shopping bag for our groceries. And if any of these things go wrong, we struggle to fix them ourselves. Instead, we wave a magic wand called a credit card and an expert will, we hope, fix it for us.

An educated person in the medieval era knew perhaps 10% of the sum of human knowledge. If human knowledge has doubled every 20 years for just the last 300 years, then the sum of human knowledge is more than 30000 times greater today. No-one can keep up. Each of us can only know a tiny fraction of all human knowledge. So even if we are better educated than the medieval peasant, we are relatively more ignorant: we know relatively less of the sum of human knowledge. Our relative ignorance grows as the sum of human knowledge grows. We are islands of expertise in an ocean of knowledge.

The benefits of increasing collective knowledge are massive for everyone: from dental and medical care, air conditioning, movies, cars, flight and telecommunications we have a lifestyle that even the greatest kings of the past would not have imagined. Knowledge is unlikely to go backwards. Our knowledge today will be the elementary building blocks of the collective knowledge which our descendants will enjoy. They will look back at our somewhat prim-itive ways in much the same way we look back at medieval peasants and wonder how they survived.

The advance of capitalism has gone hand in hand with the advance of knowledge. Capitalism has been described as a great soup of private know-how dispersed among specialist participants. As knowledge has grown, so has specialisation: as individuals we know more about less. The challenge for both firms and individuals is how to manage this exponential increase in collective knowl-edge, which no individual can keep up with. Deeper collaboration across wider networks of knowledge is essential. Knowledge specialisation and collaboration are changing the way firms and individuals work. Just as individuals are becoming ever more specialised in their skills, so too are firms. The specialist firm is the very opposite of the highly integrated firm, characterised by Ford 100 years ago. Instead of being integrated, firms are dis-integrating.

The disintegrating firm: collaborating and specialising for knowledge

Increasing specialisation is a trend which is unlikely to go away. Firms cannot expect to be good at every activity within their value chain. Just as countries benefit from the principle of comparative advantage (Scotland does not need to grow grapes for wine, when it can trade whisky for wine), so firms benefit from comparative advantage. Not every firm can, or needs to, be outstanding at IT. There are plenty of firms who specialise in IT: because they specialise, they know the current best practices, they know where to access the best skills, software and hardware, and they are committed to constantly updating the skills of their staff. There is no reason a shoe manufacturer should have the same IT capability. Specialisation is the obvious result.

Firms can no longer be like medieval walled cities: they draw strength from the power of their network, not from the height of their walls. They have gone from being closed to being open networks. This is a fundamental transformation which is still in progress: we can expect to see firms opening up more and creating wider and deeper networks. Instead of integrating the entire value chain within the firm, firms are disintegrating and focusing on one part of the value chain. When Ford started his production revolution he integrated the entire value chain, all the way from owning the forests to produce the wood for his cars to controlling the distributors who sold the cars. Competitive advantage no longer comes from integration: it comes from focus. In guru-speak, focus has become called core competences. The essence of a core competence is deep expertise in one area which can be used to build advantage across a range of markets. Honda's competence in engines (cars, motorbikes, lawn mowers, outboard motors) is often quoted as an example.

You do not need fancy theory to build advantage through knowledge, focus or core competences. Successful firms are doing this naturally. For instance, the Gore Company discovered that PTFE (polytetrafluoroethylene) had some interesting physical properties when treated: it was water repellent, especially at cooler temperatures; it was nonreactive and it had very low friction (0.1 relative to polished steel). From deep specialisation in one polymer, Gore has built a \$2 billion global business which encompasses everything from outdoor waterproof clothing to cable assemblies and piping for the aerospace industry. Deep specialisation and knowledge become practical propositions where there is global scale.

Such deep specialisation has its risks. From a competitive perspective, all niche players are at risk from a new entrant who comes up with a better mousetrap. Gore faces the might of Du Pont competing over the same polymer, PTFE, from which it derived Teflon. It also faces low cost competition as its patents run out. To stay ahead, it has to keep innovating and deepening its knowledge of how to use PTFE.

Competitively, firms have to build knowledge: they have to innovate and bring new ideas to market. These are not just scientific ideas. They can be know-how ideas. Much of the value of consulting firms lies in the know-how that they bring to the table. Unless they can constantly refresh that know-how, their skills will become obsolete rapidly. There are essentially three ways of innovating and bringing new ideas to market:

1. Top down innovation: designed innovation
2. Internal collaboration: innovation as discovery
3. External collaboration: innovation through a network

Knowledge creation and innovation has moved from top down innovation to external collaboration: this is another part of the management revolution. Knowledge creation has been turned inside out (from internal to external) and upside down (from top down to all round). Some organisations have made the transition, others are still stuck in the nineteenth century. We will look briefly at the first two, and then more fully at the third approach.

Top down innovation
Top down innovation and knowledge creation is the natural child of the Enlightenment. It assumes that wise people investigate a problem and design a solution. It is a model which has worked incredibly well. Scientific and medical advances owe much to people like Isaac Newton and Dr John Snow, who found that cholera was carried in water, not by air. But as the body of human knowledge grows, it becomes ever harder for a few wise people to know all the answers. Within a firm, top down innovation is hitting some fundamental barriers:

Risk aversion mitigates against innovation: no-one gets fired for missing an opportunity or quietly killing an idea. Plenty of people find themselves fired or posted to the corporate equivalent of cleaning toilets in Siberia if they take a risk and it does not work out.

Risk aversion is reinforced by bureaucracy: it is simply too hard to gain all the required approvals to innovate. The natural reaction of any bureaucrat is to offer advice, in the form of questions which highlight the problems of the new idea. New ideas are routinely helped to death.

No-one at the top can know all the issues, opportunities and ideas. The typical marketplace is too large and too complicated. No-one has a monopoly on wisdom or thinking. However, some organisations still work this way. Government ministers and civil servants innovate policies on the basis that somehow they think they know best. Disaster and gross mis-spending is the normal result of such arrogance. Socialist thinking in government is mirrored by corporatist thinking in some private sector firms which still operate on the nineteenth century belief that the boss knows best.

Clearly, there are exceptions where top down innovation still works. The most glaring exception is the world of the entrepreneur. This is where an individual, or a small team, sets out with a big idea and even bigger ambition. When it works, the entrepreneurs are hailed as geniuses. More often, entrepreneurs fail. This implies that great innovations are not designed: they are discovered through the brutal test of the market. Even the great entrepreneurs, who succeed with one great idea, rarely find a second great idea. If they really had cracked the innovation formula, we would expect to see them succeed more than once. We should applaud entrepreneurs for their courage and determination, but should not assume they have cracked innovation. Not even entrepreneurs have a monopoly on wisdom or ideas. In the knowledge economy, top down designed innovation is becoming an increasingly weak force.

Internal innovation: innovation as discovery

A firm is a thousand islands of expertise: to succeed, the firm's network of knowledge and skill has to work together. This leads us straight into another feature of the organisational revolution of our time: the firm has to move from command and control to a place of collaboration and commitment. No longer is the boss meant to have all the answers: the boss has to orchestrate the discovery of the solution. That means working with staff, peers and partners inside and beyond the firm. It is a fundamentally new way of working.

This means that knowledge management is not a separate function that resides with a CKO (chief knowledge officer) as was the fad of a few years ago, when gurus started pushing the knowledge economy and knowledge based firm. Firms cannot afford to isolate knowledge into a department any more than they can isolate quality into a quality department: knowledge and quality are whole firm efforts. The role of a knowledge officer is to mobilise and integrate knowledge creation across the firm.

In its most primitive form, knowledge management exists as a knowledge base on the web, or as corporate yellow pages. This is better than nothing. It allows good ideas to bubble up from across the firm. It reduces reliance on formal innovation processes. And it identifies what knowledge exists, and who owns it. The knowledge which is most useful is often tacit knowledge (know-how) rather than explicit knowledge (know what). Tacit knowledge requires working with people, not working with the web. That leads straight into the problems of global coordination and integration: even if the knowledge is there, little incentive exists for knowledge owners to invest discretionary time in helping other business units and functions build on that knowledge.

The evidence of firms codifying knowledge and best practice is mixed, at best. Technical knowledge which is used for a stable process or product can be codified. For instance, the knowledge that goes into a new pharmaceutical cannot just be codified: it can be patented. The problem is that explicit knowledge, unless it can be patented, can be copied. If it is copied by an Asian firm with labour rates just 10% of Western rates, then there is likely to be only one winner. In financial services it takes a few hours to reverse engineer the brilliant new product which one bank has just presented to a client. To stay ahead in the knowledge race, firms must either:

- innovate faster than their rivals;
- protect knowledge through patents;
- develop know-how skills which are hard to copy.

Clearly, some firms such as pharmaceutical companies are set up as product development machines which then enjoy patent protection. Most firms do not enjoy patent protection for their markets. This leaves them only two other ways of competing through knowledge. One is to innovate faster than the competition. This is extremely hard to sustain if the entire burden of innovation is carried internally. Much internal innovation fails, for the same reason that top down innovation fails: excess risk aversion and death by a helpful bureaucracy. The traditional solution is to create a skunk works which is outside the formal hierarchy of the firm: it can innovate fast without the normal restraints and fear that kills internal innovation

In practice, it is often better to look outside the firm for knowledge, solutions and innovation. External partners may already have overcome the initial barriers, built a prototype and gained market-place exposure for their idea. Much of the initial design and development will have been done. Increasingly, firms are looking to their networks for knowledge, ideas and innovation. Knowledge tsars are no longer inward facing, but outward looking. External innovation is covered in the section below.

The third option is to build distinctive know-how, which is harder to copy. Know-how can be anything from effective Total Quality Management (TQM) through to sharing of best practices and know-how in a professional services firm. The challenge is not just capturing the knowledge, but disseminating it. The experience of most professional firms is that there are a few individuals and countries that provide all the input. Typically the main contributors follow a familiar order: the United States, then the UK, then the rest of Europe and finally the rest of the world. This has two adverse effects. First, the innovation and the knowledge from the rest of the world is not fully captured. Second, the dominance of the Anglo-Saxons leads to the "not invented here" syndrome across the rest of the world, who become sceptical of the whole knowledge exercise.

Know-how does not reside in systems, it resides in people. For this reason the most effective knowledge management does not involve systems, knowledge bases and knowledge tsars. It involves HR moving people around the world on a project, assignment or even expatriate basis. This is expensive, but it is the best way to move ideas: the owner of the idea is forced to adapt the idea to local conditions and the locals are more likely to overcome their scepticism when they see the idea in practice and in person.

External collaboration: innovation through a network

Specialisation does not succeed in a vacuum: it only succeeds as part of a network. This means that the nature of the firm is changing fundamentally. If the firm no longer does everything in-house, it needs to build a new set of capabilities to make the most of its network of knowledge and capabilities. The focus of the firm is shifting from internal control to external collaboration. There are at least five ways in which firms are leveraging the power of knowledge networks:

- creating alliances in which the distinctions between competitor and partner become blurred;
- using acquisitions to build knowledge, not just scale;
- choosing where to focus along the value chain, and then partnering with other organisations to deliver the rest of the value chain;
- working with suppliers as partners, not simply vendors;
- co-creating and collaborating with customers to innovate.

Below we look at examples of each of these knowledge networks.

Creating alliances in which the distinctions between competitor and partner become increasingly blurred

P&G's Connect and Develop programme actively searches for technology to bring in and to export, with competitors as well as partners. At any one time they will actively search their network for highly specific solutions such as moisture release technology, topical products or ingredients to suppress pain during epilation and disposable stain removers. It also uses alliances to develop process technology. For instance, its "Reliability Technology" is the result of work with the Los Alamos National Laboratory. Reliability Technology is now used in 150 P&G plants globally and saves the firm over $1 billion annually. P&G not only brings technology in, but exports technology to other firms, including competitors. It has licensed out Nodax which is a technology that enables the creation of new biopolymers from renewable sources. P&G is not a plastics manufacturer, so Meredian is better placed to exploit it. By active use of a broad network, P&G is able to focus its efforts on building knowledge leadership in a few areas which matter most to it.

Using acquisitions to build knowledge, not just scale
IBM has made 60 acquisitions between 2004 and 2008 for a modest $20 billion. The acquisitions were not about scale. They were about building knowledge in a few target areas: storage and security, cloud computing, business intelligence and trading processes. Even IBM recognised that it did not have all the resources to build this knowledge internally. It is better and quicker to buy the proven knowledge in.

Choosing where to compete along the value chain
Apple's iPod is responsible for the employment of 27 000 people outside the US. Only 300 of those work for Apple. 19 000 of them are working for partner organisations making hard drives, display modules, processor chips, computer chips and assembling all the parts. Another 8000 are in partner firms in retailing, engineering and professional services. Apple is still responsible for the iPod, even although it focuses on a small part of the value chain.

Working with suppliers as partners, not simply vendors
As firms specialise along the value chain, they become more dependent on the expertise of the rest of the value chain. No longer are suppliers simply providers of simple commodities which can be competitively bid out. Increasingly, suppliers are an essential part of both the supply chain and the knowledge, design and innovation chain. For instance:

- Auto manufacturers are reducing the number of suppliers: they want fewer but deeper and more collaborative relationships with key suppliers. Bain & Co estimated that the total number of Tier 1 suppliers will reduce from 600 to 30 over the period 2002 to 2010.
- Frost & Sullivan estimate that the global IT outsourcing market is $1430 billion in 2009. This represents a huge leap of faith by firms who are entrusting much of their core operations to a third party. IT partners have expertise which most firms cannot and will not develop. This is a skills based partnership in which the traditional buyer–vendor relationship is turned upside down: the buyer depends on the vendor more than the other way around. The traditional, adversarial buy and sell model has to be replaced with a longer term partnership based on trust.
- Apple's iPhone is made much more attractive by the many third party applications which are designed for it: instead of keeping the iPhone as an entirely proprietary product, Apple gains strength from making it an open platform for other partners to exploit.

Treating customers as partners
Using them to help innovate and identify new opportunities. This is the land of co-creation, promoted by Venkat Ramaswamy and

others at Michigan Business School. It proposes that the critical knowledge partnership, and source of innovation, is the customer. Traditionally, market innovation has been a matter of trial and error in which the producer attempts to understand and respond to the perceived needs of the customer. International Flavors and Fragrances have turned that problem on its head. They have removed the guesswork by letting the customers design the product to their needs. IFF produce flavours to help food manufacturers: a web application linked to a machine allows key customers to create and test their own flavours automatically.

All of these trends follow the same pattern. They all involve successful firms opening themselves up and exploiting the wider network of knowledge to which they belong. Firms cannot succeed as an island: they can only succeed as part of a network. The skills needed to make a network work are different from the skills needed in a command and control, integrated firm. Collaboration, changed attitudes to risk and to innovation become more important. Equally, there has to be discipline and focus which comes from strategic clarity of purpose. Once a firm opens itself up to a network, there will be an excess of opportunities and a deficit of management capacity to exploit all those opportunities. The job of management is to focus the network on the biggest opportunities.

The knowledge economy and the knowledge worker

Just as firms are becoming islands of specialisation in networks of knowledge and capability, so too are managers. Managers are becoming ever more specialised in their skills. For instance, 25 years ago a management consultant might legitimately work, in one year, on telecoms, petrochemicals, private health care and banking doing strategic, change, organisational and operational work in countries from Saudi Arabia through Europe to America. Now, clients expect specialist expertise from their advisors. One consultant found himself spending a year doing nothing more than building business cases to justify IT programmes for UK life assurance companies. By the end of the year, he was the world expert in such an arcane art, which meant that the firm wanted him to stick with his expertise. So much for career development.

Staff specialisation has high value to the firm, but can be a huge bear trap for the staff. Deep specialisation does little to build the general management skills required to run a business. Even the progression from skilled specialist to front line supervisor is a hurdle which many talented specialists cannot leap: the skill sets are simply different. Technical skills are important for success as a specialist book keeper, systems analyst or accountant. If the specialist wants to become a manager, the specialist skills become less important relative to people and political skills. For the firm, this raises the challenge of building the right skills for the future. Specialist knowledge is valuable: it is essentially explicit knowledge or "Know-what skills" that can be codified in books, courses and knowledge banks. Many management skills are about tacit knowledge: "know-how" skills which depend deeply on context and personal style. These are harder to put in a manual and are typically not learned from books or courses.

Tacit skills are discovered through good or poor personal experience, and by observing the experience of others: peers, role models and bosses. This means that the nature of skills development is changing, although the change is happening too slowly to satisfy the expectations of many managers (see the chapter on Management). The old model consisted of a trainer with a flip chart and a franchised theory holding court. But if people like to learn from each other, not from a theory, then it makes sense to help staff learn that way. Instead of training people, the focus is switching to helping people discover what works for them in context. That means more structured projects and experience, more coaching and mentoring, more peer to peer workshops and best practice development and much less formal training. This sort of knowledge development is far harder to orchestrate than simply buying a vendor who has an original perspective and an entertaining style.

The problem for managers is that the knowledge which represents management theory is not very useful, and is often very dangerous. Existing frameworks for strategy, finance, leadership and accounting are either deficient or misleading. Many managers will claim that they are practical and not influenced by the intellectual and academic nonsense that comes out of business schools. Keynes, the great economist, would disagree. He observed: "Practical men, who believe themselves to be quite exempt from any intellectual influences, are usually the slaves of some defunct economist." Managers are often unconsciously slaves to simplistic formulas which have their origins in business schools or consulting firms.

The knowledge which managers need most and value most comes from judgement, experience and focus. It is personal experience about what works in context. But neither managers nor firms can rely on the long, random walk of experience for building leaders and knowledge. There has to be some structure to the learning journey. Effective knowledge management will put structure on the learning journey of individuals and will contextualise that learning for them. Existing frameworks can be used as building blocks in the journey of discovery, but they cannot be used as substitutes for personal discovery. This represents a radical departure from traditional training programmes, but firms are only slowly understanding this.

Conclusions

The knowledge economy drives firms to specialise. They are islands of specialisation in an ocean of knowledge. This is driving firms to become more specialised along the value chain and to become more collaborative with partners within and beyond their immediate value chain. The firm has to exploit the ocean of knowledge so that it can innovate and grow successfully. Knowledge creation is no longer an internal or top down affair where wise people solve all the firm's problems. No firm or individual has a monopoly on wisdom. Firms are moving from being closed, integrated entities to being part of an open network. The firm is being turned inside out.

As with firms, so with managers. Managers are becoming more specialised in their skills, which changes the skills they need to succeed. Collaboration and networking skills are becoming more important relative to traditional command and control skills. To make things happen, managers need to harness the skills of other managers across the organisation, over whom they have no formal control.

The knowledge economy is turning the firm on its head. For a successful manager, balancing knowledge with power is more exciting and more challenging than ever before.

Chapter Seven

Organisations: From Compliance to Commitment

Thirty years ago a publishing sensation swept through management. *In Search of Excellence*, by two young McKinsey consultants, appeared to have discovered the elixir of organisational success. Their formula was distilled down to a few handy ideas that any manager could aspire to follow. This was the apex of management science.

A generation later, many of the "excellent" companies they had featured seem to have lost the formula for excellence: they have been taken over or overtaken by other less excellent companies. Many other firms have diligently searched for excellence for the last 30 years, but the prize seems as elusive as it ever was. There is a reason that excellence has proved elusive: it does not exist.

In the introduction we saw how excellent companies have a disturbing habit of falling by the wayside, and how the top firms in both the USA and the UK have a half life of 20 years: every 20 years we can expect half of the great companies to go bust or get taken over. Too many firms go from good to great to bust, like Circuit City and Fannie Mae (both profiled in *Good to Great*). Perhaps greatness and excellence are not the right thing for us to be looking for.

The experience of most managers in most firms is not one of unqualified excellence. The firm's global headquarters always look impressive from the outside: imposing monuments of chrome, glass and steel. Inside, the reality is a little more mundane. The day to day reality for most managers involves a mountain of emails, routine meetings, chasing people, managing misunderstandings, averting mini crises, scrambling to meet deadlines and deliverables, negotiating the politics of making things happen and trying to keep personal and professional lives in balance. This is a reality far removed from the breathless, gushing perfection which each new guru promises with their instant success formula.

Far from getting better, things may be getting harder from cubicle land to the rarified atmosphere of the executive suite. The old certainties of organisational life are being replaced by a new age of uncertainty, ambiguity and opportunity. Traditional functional structures offered a world of certainty, clarity and conformity. It is a world which still exists in some of the slower moving machine bureaucracies of the world, from central government to the life assurance industry. Elsewhere, it is a disappearing world. Machine bureaucracies at their best are guided by the twin stars of fairness and efficiency. At their worst, they become rule bound, inefficient and inflexible monsters which respond neither to the market nor to change.

If the old adage is to be believed, organisations enable ordinary people to achieve extraordinary things. In practice, the reverse is often true. Many organisations make extraordinary people achieve ordinary things. People who have energy, ambition and creativity in supporting their community and family leave that talent and energy at home. Making the most of people's talents is not a new challenge for a firm. What is new is that the challenge is becoming much harder and the way that the firm responds is having to change. At the heart of the challenge is the need to move from a compliance to a commitment culture. Firms preach about passion, delegation and having a vision and values. What firms practice is not the same as what they preach. The reality is that firms are showing less trust, not more trust in staff. Technology allows managers to achieve ever finer control and deeper knowledge of exactly who is doing what, where and when. Technology, combined with a fetish for targets, means that there is more control than ever before. The challenge is to balance the power of technology with the power of people: technology needs to enable people, not control them. But making the technology and the people work together is becoming harder, not easier.

Making organisations work is getting harder for four main reasons:

- Increasing efficiency, represented by re-engineering, has thinned out management ranks at the same time as making organisations more complex for managers who now have to manage across functions (processes) as well as within functions.
- Increasing need for flexibility to adapt to customer, competitor and technological change.
- Increasing globalisation and fragmentation of the value chain: most of the resources required of a manager existed within the

firm, and were often local. Now key resources may be outsourced and even if they are in the firm, they may be located
anywhere in the world.

- Increasing skills and power of employees mean the employees
  tend to be higher value and higher maintenance. The compliance culture of the old hierarchy is disappearing: building
  a high commitment culture is much harder work (rewards,
  measures, commitment, mission, values etc.).

Perhaps because management is so hard, managers are easily
seduced by the soothsayers who offer them a simple formula to
achieve excellence and greatness. These business gurus are like
fortune tellers: they know the answer even if they do not know the
question. And they will promise you a great fortune in the future,
for which they will charge you a great fortune in the present. In
this revolution all the rules and certainties of the past have been
overturned. We cannot know all the answers and know the future.
Instead, we must understand the challenges which the revolution
presents. There are three main challenges:

- Searching for fit and balance, not for excellence formulas
- Managing a world of increasing complexity, scale and
  globalisation
- Moving from compliance to commitment and managing the
  structural revolution

This chapter explores each of these questions and suggests some
solutions.

The end of excellence: the search for fit and balance

Practising managers have long realised that there is a huge gap between the hype of excellence and day to day reality. In reality excellence is a mirage which exists only in the minds of the gurus. The main problems with the focus on excellence or greatness are:

- Excellence is the wrong goal for a firm: profits, sustainability, market share are all possible goals. Excellence is like virtue, wisdom and charity. It is nice if you have it, but it does not necessarily mean you increase your market share next quarter.
- The search for excellence or greatness either becomes an exercise in hubris, or else becomes thoroughly demoralising as managers discover the gap in their performance versus the ideal which can never be achieved. Like penniless window shoppers at Christmas time, the knowledge that there is something better which you cannot have is of little comfort.
- Excellent and great firms fall by the wayside in much the same way as less excellent firms: if there is a formula for success, excellence is not the right formula.

Just to re-emphasise the point, take a look at what happened to the firms which had been identified after meticulous research by Tom Peters and Robert Waterman in *In Search of Excellence* and in *Good to Great* by Jim Collins. *Business Week* noted in 1984 that one third of the 43 excellent companies identified by Peters and Waterman were in financial difficulty within five years of the research being conducted. And their list of high tech firms included companies such as: Atari, Data General, DEC, Lanier, NCR and Wang. They have all found their way onto the scrap heap of history. If they were excellent, who wants excellence?

Good to Great is more recent, so there has been less time for fate to take its toll. Nevertheless, since 2001 this is what has happened to some of his eleven "Great" firms:

- Circuit City: went bust in 2009
- Gillette, taken over by P&G in 2005
- Nucor, profit warning 2009
- Fannie Mae: $100 billion tax payer bail out 2008–9

If the consequence of greatness is to get bailed out, go bust or be taken over, most managers would live happily without greatness. Managers need something more practical than theories of excellence and greatness.

To understand what managers should look for, try the following exercise. Design the perfect sports star or perfect animal. Here is what perfection might look like:

- The perfect animal (predator): the jaws of an crocodile, ears of an elephant, neck of a giraffe, wings of an eagle, tail of a scorpion, legs of a cheetah, the hide of a rhino and attitude of a hippo. The perfect animal will promptly collapse under the weight of its own improbability.
- The perfect sports star: the height of a basketball star, the eye of an archer, the smile of a synchronised swimmer, the arms of a shot putter, the body of a weight lifter, the lungs of an oarsman,

the legs of a sprinter and the feet of a footballer. This perfect sports star will win nothing.

Now try to design the perfect organisation. Like the perfect sports star or perfect animal, the perfect organisation is not a mish mash of different bits of different firms who seem to be doing well at the moment. Think again about some excellent animals or great sports stars. In each case, they are very well adapted to their particular environment or sport. Reindeer survive in very hostile arctic conditions which the lion hates: put the reindeer into the African bush and the lions would be happier than if they had to survive in the Arctic. Equally, great sports stars tend to be great in one sport: weight lifters are not great sprinters who rarely make good marathon runners who tend to make little impact in American football. There are exceptions, but the rule is that excellence is highly specific to one environment or one sport.

Instead of searching for excellence, we need to search for fit: we need to find what works for us in our environment today. This is why companies come and go – it's not because they don't have the magic dust, it's just that what they do stops working. What works in one industry may not work in another. For instance, successful entrepreneurs understand and even embrace risk: risk spells opportunity. Go into central government and risk is like kryptonite to the civil servants: risk spells threat. So is the perfect organisation one that embraces risk or avoids risk? Well, it depends where you are and what you do. Risk appetite, and even the meaning of risk, varies from industry to industry.

The figure below illustrates in simplified form the organisational forms of two types of firm: investment banking which appeared to be wildly successful until the implosion of the credit crunch, and a manufacturer of branded detergents.

	Investment bank	Branded detergents
Culture	Hunters	Farmers
Structure	Team profit centres	Functional – marketing-led
Scope	Conflicts of interest	Complex value chain
Systems, measures	Profit vs. risk management	Market share vs. profits
Skills	Hire and fire	Build and grow internally

The fundamental difference between the bank and the manufac-turer is between hunting and farming. The hunter has a short term view, you eat what you kill, it has heroes and (increasingly) villains, teams are small and there is huge conflict between the team (max-imise profit, whatever the risk) and the shareholder. It is a winner-takes-all world: winners make their fortunes and the unlucky or incompetent lose their jobs. This simplified summary of the invest-ment bank also highlights their fatal flaw: the culture of risk and the systems of control were not in balance. It is not enough for an organisation to fit with the external environment. It must also balance internally: culture, systems, skills, measures must be aligned.

The manufacturer is the opposite of the bank: it farms instead of hunts. It has a longer time horizon focused on building a sustain-able customer franchise with high market share. Although market-ing and brands lead the functional organisation, cooperation is essential: brands will cooperate to minimise internal competition and a high degree of coordination is required across functions and with external suppliers and customers to go to market successfully. The need for cooperation and coordination requires building a management team who know from experience how to make things happen across a very complex organisation. Hiring and firing is not the way to build that experience. Instead, this firm promotes 100% from within.

Advising firms that they need to achieve fit and balance is both more liberating and more complicated than offering eight nifty phrases which will transform them into excellent companies. Managers should not follow a formula. They must create their own success formula: that is partly why management has been and always will be both demanding and exciting. There are no set rules.

Even when not searching for excellence, firms are encouraged to copy best practice. This is as dangerous as searching for excellence. Firms which copy best practice are, by definition, followers not leaders. By the time they achieve best practice, the leader will have moved on. Best practice means competing on the same terms as someone else who is already better than you: that is a perfect recipe for underachievement.

For example, in the 1980s the West finally discovered that Japan was a threat. So it decided to copy Japanese best practice. This was an exercise which doomed the auto industry to failure. Copying a little bit of TQM, or *kaizen* or any other technique is like doing a little bit of a heart transplant. To succeed, you need to do it all or not at all. Even worse, early attempts to copy Japanese techniques were based on very flawed understandings of how the techniques really worked: the heart transplant was being done with only part of the manual by a surgeon who had never done it before. Copying Japan was not a great success. Each time the West thought it had caught up, Japan had moved on. Whatever else Japan may be good or bad at, it is world class at being Japanese; a gold medallist in eating sushi, bowing and doing TQM. The West was never going to beat Japan at being Japanese and copying sushi, bowing and TQM. Competitive advantage does not come from following the leader: it comes from being different in a relevant way.

Ricardo Semler shows how far you can move from management orthodoxy and be successful. His company, Semco, is in the traditional business of pumps and other industrial equipment. But Semco's organisation is anything but traditional or orthodox. He takes participative management to an extreme. Workers set their own hours and pay; hire and assess their supervisors; there are no offices for managers. The start of the transformation to a participative company came with the company canteen. Workers were always complaining about it. Semler listened, and then handed control of the canteen over to the workers. The complaints stopped. From there, participation grew to letting workers choose the colour of their uniforms and the paint for their walls. The more discretion they gained, the better they performed. The result is a business which has easily withstood Semler's five-month absence after a horrific car crash in 2005.

The message from Semco is not that managers should all freak out and let the workers take control, although that could make progress for many firms. The message is that any form of organisation can succeed, provided it fits the environment and is balanced internally.

Managing complexity and coordination, especially in a global firm

Building an effective organisation is becoming harder, not easier. As firms grow in size and complexity, so the challenges of coordination grow. Firms are becoming more complicated for two reasons: the rise of the global firm and re-engineering.

The rise of the global firm and global supply chain

Globalisation is increasingly happening within firms: instead of exporting and importing with foreign partners, many firms are creating self-contained global value chains. Key parts of the value chain will be in-house. OECD estimates that in 1999 46.7% of all US imports came through intra-firm trade. This proportion rises to over 70% in trade with Japan: Japanese companies no longer simply export, but they control the value chain all the way through to the American customer. Between 1990 and 1999 intra-firm trade between Japan and the rest of Asia more than doubled for both imports and exports as Japanese manufacturers controlled their supply chain back towards manufacturers in Asia as well as forwards to American customers. They have created in-house global value chains in key industries such as auto manufacturing and consumer electronics. They may do the design in Japan and manufacture a few key components there; then they have assembly done in a low cost Asian subsidiary before exporting to a wholly owned subsidiary in America. This is a pattern which American companies are also following. Over 70% of American imports from Ireland are based on intra-firm trade. Companies like Dell use Ireland as a reliable place to assemble goods for sale in America: like the Japanese, they have created an in-house global value chain.

Just as manufacturing firms coordinate value chains around the world, so do professional service firms. Manufacturers move product around the world: professional service firms move people and skills around the world. This leads to organisational complexity. It is now commonplace for large professional service firms such as Accenture to be organised around a mixture of functions (technology, change, outsourcing), geography (Asia, Americas, EMEA), industry groups (transport and travel, financial services, public sector) and customers. Serving a global customer requires integrating skills from around the world and from different functional groups.

The logic of moving from import–export to in-house global value chains may be impeccable. Making it work is much harder. There is plenty of technology to help: enterprise software and supply chain integration software help integrate transactions across the supply chain. Emails and video conferencing help management communications. And yet the constant refrain with most global firms is that they find making globalisation work hard work. Plenty of work has been done to study global firms at a high level: but the problems are not with the high level architecture of the global firm. Solutions tend to be highly generic and focus on how far to decentralise or centralise (Bartlett & Ghoshal, *Managing Across Borders* 2002). The problem is more practical: how do we get teams of people working virtually across borders?

The challenge of the cross border team is not about communication or protocols: most firms have plenty of protocols and technology. The real problems are about trust, power, belonging and identity. If I am working in America and my boss is in France, where all the decisions are made and I rarely get to see the boss, I will be uncomfortable. I will not feel in control of my destiny, I will not feel part of the team, I will not know how to get things done and how to influence the boss I seldom see. I will have little sense of belonging, loyalty or commitment. These worries represent the front line challenges of globalisation which practising managers experience.

In-house globalisation creates a set of challenges which management are still trying to overcome. The technology for integrating transactions across the globe exists. But technology does not integrate people. People have a need to belong, and belonging to a virtual group that is spread across the world is not something that is in human nature: we do not have much experience of it. An early, and highly successful, example was the Roman Empire which lasted for hundreds of years longer than most global firms will, and without any of the technology which modern firms benefit from. When Pontius Pilate left Rome to govern the troublesome province of Judea, he could not be controlled by email, video conference and tight reporting around monthly variances in the salt tax. He had to resolve challenges personally without a quick global conference call to get advice and share responsibility and spread the blame. If delegation meant crucifying the wrong person, well …woops!

Empires from the past offer insights to business empires of today around how to control and coordinate globally: the ancient empires were able to do so without email, phones or the video conferencing. Instead, they forged a common culture among a small elite. The elite will have grown and developed together acquiring common values and skills. The foibles, strengths and weaknesses of each member of the elite were well known to the others. There were high levels of personal trust, until a power struggle for the succession emerged. Then there would be plotting, skulduggery and assassinations. Modern global organisations emulate the plotting, skulduggery and career assassinations of the ancient empires. They could usefully emulate the more positive aspects of the ancient empires: invest in developing a cohesive, trusted elite with common values, experiences and outlook. This is lousy in terms of true diversity: it implies that whatever race, sex or faith you may be you should sign up to the corporate way of doing things. But when it comes to making things happen, building trust, making decisions, managing ambiguity and managing remote teams, then intimacy beats diversity every time.

From compliance to commitment: the structural revolution

Revolutions often involve the world being turned upside down. For a while, it seemed that the structure of the firm was going to be turned upside down. The old organisation structure with the boss at the top and the workers at the bottom was turned upside down to show the boss at the bottom and the front line workers at the top, interacting with customers who had never before appeared on any organisation chart. To the boss, this showed that he was humble, serving the staff and focused on customers. It made a good speech for the boss. Unfortunately, what the boss said and what the audience heard were quite different. What the audience saw (see Figures 7.1(a) and (b)) was a spinning top out of control where the boss pretended to be carrying the entire organisation on his shoulders. And most front line workers did not care to be patronised by the pretence that they were at the top of the organisation.

In practice, the structural revolution is more far reaching and more complicated than simply turning the pyramid on its head. The pyramid has been turned on its side (Figure 7.1(c)) and has been completely reconfigured. The simplicity and certainty of the functional organisation has given way to the complexity of a multi-dimensional matrix in which processes can count as much as functions. For instance, we have already seen how Accenture formally has three dimensions to its organisation: geography, function and industry group. In practice, teams organise around individual

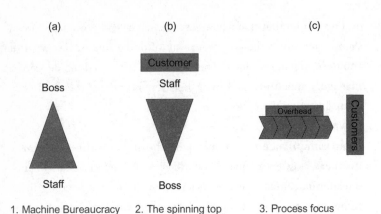

Figure 7.1 Three views of the organisation

clients who represent a fourth dimension. Managing your career or making things happen in such a complex web becomes an exotic art form which requires a new set of skills. The chapter on Management shows that political skills are becoming essential to successful management: these are skills that are not taught formally either at business school or on company courses.

Many firms do not bother with a formal organisation chart, and for good reason. Most organisation charts are out of date by the time they are published. They simply make work for staffers. Staff may enjoy putting people in boxes on their organisation chart, but preferably people should not be put in boxes until they are dead. And whatever the formal organisation may show, that is not how the organisation actually works. Figure 7.1(c), the sideways or process view of the organisation, is closer to the operating reality of most firms. The firm is a series of activities along a value chain which eventually delivers a good or a service to a customer.

The job of line managers, operating in the value chain, is to coordinate with other managers across the value chain to make progress. Managers glue the value chain together: in the old world, managers glued the different levels of the hierarchy together. Managers now have to work in three dimensions: not only up and down the hierarchy, but also across the value chain. The value chain is then enabled, controlled or obstructed by various staff and overhead functions such as IT, HR, Legal and Health & Safety. The formal organisation structure may show a traditional functional hierarchy or a complex matrix: but the operating reality is one of attempting to coordinate across departments in other parts of the organisation. That is where political skills become essential: managers have to make things happen with people over whom they have no control.

The informal, process view of organisation has huge advantages over the traditional, formal functional view of organisations. In a functionally organised firm, work is clear, simple and focused. But integration and coordination are weak: work tends to get thrown over the wall from one functional silo to another. If there are problems, then they get escalated up and down the hierarchy rather than being resolved at the front line. As a result, decision making is slow and the firm finds it hard to be responsive and flexible to the market. The process driven firm is more complicated and more ambiguous. When it works it is flexible, nimble and market focused. When it does not work it becomes a political rats' nest.

The challenge is to make the current style of organisation work. Many firms manage new style structures with old style systems, then they wonder why it does not work. To make the informal, process driven organisation work requires re-thinking how to manage the following:

1.   Systems: rewards, measures and controls
2.   Staffing: skills, development and recruitment
3.   Culture: values, belonging and purpose
4.   Structures: integration and coordination

We will briefly explore each of these challenges.

Systems, rewards and measures

This takes us straight into an age old debate about the nature of people. If you believe people are fundamentally lazy, untrustworthy and will do the minimum required to avoid sanctions, then you are a follower of Theory X. If you believe people are capable and committed and simply need to be encouraged and directed, then you believe in Theory Y. Theories X and Y were outlined by Douglas MacGregor in *The Human Side of Enterprise* in 1964. The two beliefs lead in opposite directions in terms of control and measures. Theory X leads straight to short spans of control, tight measurement, clear sanctions and rewards for performance and a strict hierarchy. The nineteenth century sweatshop, and some modern call centres, fit this description well. Theory Y leads us to a world of trust, empowerment and delegation, towards Richard Semler's Semco, where employee democracy has taken over. Semco trusts its employees even to determine their own pay and working hours. Most firms say they trust their staff (Theory Y) but their systems say they prefer Theory X. Semco is seen as an amusing, but dangerous and anarchic, example of success.

Theory X depends on having clear command and control and clearly defined work to measure. However, work is becoming harder to measure: we can measure how many cars roll off a production line, but measuring the productivity of someone in cubicle land is far harder. Work is much more ambiguous. It requires more integration and cooperation with other departments: who did what is less than clear when it comes to assessing performance.

The evidence is that firms can be bolder in moving to Theory Y. P&G had a very traditional manufacturing plant in Chicago in the 1980s, with adversarial relations between management and workers. They faced a critical competition to win the firm's mandate to manufacture a new product. Management made the radical decision to leave the plant and let the workers figure out how they would win the pitch. Productivity soared, they won the pitch and management had to negotiate their way back into the plant after a few weeks. Moving from control to commitment can have dramatic results.

Staffing and skills
Even in recession, there is a much publicised "war for talent". First, we need to understand what sort of talent is critical to success. Typically, managers think of the war for talent as being the hunt for the best technical talent. Technical ability is important, but other skills are becoming more important. Think about how many people get fired for their lack of technical competence: not many. The skills shortage is not about technical skills. Two other skills are becoming essential: people skills and political skills.

People skills are needed to work well with other people. Political skills are required to make things happen. The world of management has woken up to the need for more people skills, which are often dressed up as EQ (Emotional Quotient). As we move away from command and control to a commitment based workplace, people skills continue to become more important.

Political skills are less obvious but more important. Managers have to make things happen through people they do not control. That requires building alliances of trust and networks of power and influence; knowing which battles to fight and how to fight them; dealing with crises, conflicts and opposition; influencing and persuading people over whom you have no authority. These skills are essential to survival and success in any revolution, not least in the management revolution. As organisations dis-integrate, and as power fragments, so the subtle political arts become ever more important.

Firms have woken up to the need to enhance the people skills of their managers. But political skills remain uncharted territory, largely because "politics" is seen as a dirty word in most firms. It is associated with careerism, back stabbing and duplicity. But if firms want to breed managers who can make things happen, then enhancing the more positive political skills is essential.

Both people and political skills are covered further in the chapter on Management.

Values

Values are becoming more important to success. Firms know this, but they do not know what to do about it. In practice, values are often much derided, and justifiably so. Values statements which are lovingly crafted in the executive suite appear to be nonsense outside it, even after the motivational posters and speeches, the brass plaques and the corporate videos have gone out in support of the values statement. Many values statements are motherhood and apple pie which do not help staff decide what they should or should not do in ambiguous situations. For instance, here is shortened version of one leading company's value statement:

> We value integrity, honesty, openness, personal excellence, constructive self-criticism, continual self-improvement, and mutual respect ... We take on big challenges, and pride ourselves on seeing them through. We hold ourselves accountable to our customers, shareholders, partners, and employees by honoring our commitments ...

This is all worthy stuff. But is there really anyone who prefers the opposite of any of this: dishonesty, incompetence, disrespect, giving up on challenges, not being accountable to anyone? They are all fine words but give little practical guidance on what is different about this firm from any other firm.

Every firm has a set of values, which may or may not be written down. Those values are the product of four variables which any firm can manage:

- The actions of leaders, especially at moments of truth: in a crunch does the leader put profits, customers, quality or staff first? Does the leader talk about sacrifice and make personal sacrifice as well? Does the leader seek understanding and progress or does the leader seek to analyse and blame?
- Reward and measurement systems: if people are meant to be empowered and trusted, do the evaluation and control systems reflect that? Who is preferred for promotion: the high performer with dubious values or the decent performer with great values?
- Longevity of service: the longer people stay in the firm, the more the values become embedded. This is noticeable after two firms merge: even a decade later it is often very obvious who came from which firm. It takes a long time to embed values, and even longer to change them.

- Recruitment criteria: firms routinely screen for technical, intellectual and people skills. They rarely screen for values. However, perhaps the most common reason for an employee parting ways with a firm is because of a lack of fit: the culture and the values of the firm and the individual were simply too different.

Values help explain how the credit crunch came about: it was not a failure of regulation; it was a failure of values. The regulators will busily regulate the symptoms of the problem (capital adequacy, governance, risk management). But they will fail to address the cause: the values of greed and short term focus. Like treating measles with spot remover, the regulators will find that regulating the symptoms of the credit crunch will cure nothing. It will not prevent the next crisis, and you cannot regulate values.

Michael Lewis, who wrote *Liar's Poker* in 1989, exposed what he thought was the greed of Wall Street. He recalled that John Gutfreund, the CEO of Salomon Brothers, was paid an outrageous $3.1 million in 1986. That seems quaint nowadays. The average compensation for an S&P 500 CEO in 2008 was $10.4 million. The top 10 recipients of TARP bail outs received $243 billion in federal funds. The CEOs of these failed firms rewarded themselves with $247 million in compensation for their heroic failures. By comparison, Gutfreund looks like a self-denying monk. Instead of his book being taken as a morality tale against greed Lewis found, in his words: "I was knee-deep in letters from students at Ohio State who wanted to know if I had any other secrets to share about Wall Street. They'd read my book as a how-to manual." With those values, Wall Street was an accident waiting to happen.

Naturally, it is easy to be wise after the event. As one writer put it: "Banks reward loan officers on the volume of loans they make. Lending money to people is easy: getting it back is harder. By the time the bad debt mounts up, the loan officers have received their bonus and moved on." This is a statement of the obvious in light of the sub-prime crisis. Actually, that writer was me, in *How to Manage* in 2006, when bankers were still thought of as masters of the universe. The problems were obvious but when the money was rolling in, managers and regulators chose to ignore them.

Structures

There is no such thing as the perfect organisation structure. Every structure is a trade off between competing priorities:

- Centralisation can build economies of scale and deep expertise; local autonomy encourages market focus, flexibility and greater accountability.
- Clear boundaries (silos) encourage greater identity, belonging, focus and expertise but make cooperation, decision making, flexibility and innovation harder.
- Geographic, industry, customer or functional focus all work at different times for different organisations.

As firms grow and globalise, these trade offs become harder to make. Professional service firms, from consultants and accountants to law firms and movie makers, have a simple solution. In practice, they organise day to day around clients and projects. The corporate overhead of industry, geography and functional management only comes into play at a few critical events: assigning talent, spreading knowledge, deciding budgets and determining promotions. Other firms, such as manufacturers, cannot organise around a series of shortlived projects or clients. They have to make a sustainable set of trade offs.

The solution most firms come up with is to do a bit of everything, but a bit more of some things than of others. This looks extraordinarily messy, and it is. But it tends to work. As ever, practice trumps theory. Inevitably, middle managers can get weary and cynical about the constant carousel of change: the focus of the matrix goes from industry to geography to functional and back to industry focus again. What goes round comes round. To think of reorganisations as rational events which get the firm nearer to perfection misses the point. Reorganisations serve non rational purposes. They:

- demonstrate that the leader is doing something and is in control;
- move some power barons out of the way and replace them with loyal followers;
- reset the psychological contract with key executives: show that it is no longer business as usual, and that the priorities have changed;
- signal to the organisation that greater focus is required on industry markets, geographical markets or functional skills.

This may not be what is formally announced when the reorganisation is made public, but they are valid reasons for change. The net result of this is that organisation structures are probably the weakest form of achieving the integration and coordination required across the business: all that can be achieved is a trade off between imperfect solutions. Reorganisations are high profile but the lasting change comes from the less glamorous work of aligning values, skills, rewards, measures and processes.

Conclusions

The nature of the firm is changing fundamentally. Firms are specialising and globalising at the same time; they are becoming less hierarchical and more process focused; they are moving from command and control to coordination and commitment; Anglo-Saxon firms are no longer the only success models to follow. Organisations which have been held up as exemplars of success, excellence and longevity have a disturbing habit of going bust or being taken over by other less "excellent" firms. The simplistic success formulas of the past are breaking down under the onslaught of change and the impact of reality: nothing is as simple as formulas predict.

Old fashioned success formulas are not just misleading: they are dangerous. No-one can succeed by copying little bits of formulas or by tilting at windmills called excellence or greatness. As managers we have to create our own unique formula for success: we have to find out what works for us in our context today. Because the world is always changing, we find that our formula and our organisation must change as well.

The challenge for management is getting harder all the time. The scale, complexity and globalisation of business make the task of control and coordination harder than ever. Forget the search for excellence: many firms need to search for competence. Complex firms are extremely hard to maintain. Things are always going wrong. To make things go right takes huge effort.

If we free ourselves from the world of prescriptive formulas we can create organisations which are radically different, succeed and meet the expectations of a new generation: better educated, with higher potential and more demanding than ever. Not every organisation can become a Semco, but it should inspire us to have the courage to think and act differently. What works in practice is preferable to what works in theory. It is better to let the theory follow our practice, than have practice follow the theory.

Chapter Eight

Change: Why Dinosaurs Can't Dance

Darwin offers this management tip: "It is not the strongest species that survive, or the most intelligent, but the ones who are most responsive to change." The evidence of most great firms is that they struggle to change. Successful firms have a successful way of doing things which they find hard to abandon, often until it is too late. Just as a lion and a polar bear would find it hard to adapt to each other's environments, most firms find it hard to change to a new environment.

History tells us that the old regime always suffers when there is a revolution. This applies to business, not just politics. The giants of today look powerful, but they are very vulnerable to the upstarts of tomorrow. Today's giants are prisoners of past success: they are locked into a business model and cannot or will not adapt to the disruptive change which successful challengers bring. This chapter shows why incumbents are so vulnerable and why change proves so difficult.

Management is largely about change. The job of a manager is rarely to keep things exactly as they are. Managers are meant to improve things: reduce costs, raise quality, accelerate speed to market, improve processes and products, raise service levels, acquire new customers and build new markets. For most managers, the pace of change is faster than ever but for many firms, the pace of change is far too slow. To understand this paradox, we first need to understand the nature of change.

Most managers are engaged in a process of evolutionary change. Evolutionary change means optimising the firm's existing business model: use fewer resources to achieve a better outcome. Making this happen is seriously hard work. Most managers find that all of their effort is focused on keeping the machine going, not on changing it. Every firm suffers from entropy: the highly ordered state of efficiency is not natural. Things go wrong: customers change their minds, competitors get tough, some staff want more, other staff leave and have to be replaced, suppliers mess up and events happen. To maintain efficiency is hard; to make evolutionary change is far harder. Most managers prefer that revolutionary change is kept out of the workplace.

For most firms, most of the time, evolutionary change is fine. Mature industries settle down into vicious competitive stalemate. Unilever and P&G have been locked together in a global, and indecisive, household detergents war for decades. In similar fashion, major airlines, the insurance industry, auto manufacturers and pharmaceutical companies have fought out wars with broadly unchanged business models for longer than most people can remember. In each industry there has been cost reduction, quality improvements, new products and merger activity. But the fundamental nature of the industry has not changed. The main players in each industry are the same as a generation ago, although some will have merged. In these industries, the daily grind of management meets the change needs of the firm.

Increasingly, industry equilibrium is being punctuated by revolutionary change which creates new rules of survival and success. When this revolutionary change happens, incumbent firms repeatedly fail to rise to the challenge. They cannot change fast enough: they become dinosaurs, and dinosaurs don't dance.

In the chapter on strategy we saw how traditional incumbents have become usurped by new challengers. The incumbents had all the advantages: money, resources, skills, market access. And yet they have been threatened by upstarts who were not even on their competitive radar screen.

The move to the new world disorder is not an orderly and predictable progression of change. Some industries experience modest change; other industries experience rapid and disruptive change. This raises some basic questions about how managers can cope with change. The main themes we will address in this change chapter are:

- the nature of disruptive or revolutionary change: why incumbents are always vulnerable;
- why firms struggle with evolutionary change;
- how managers cope with change personally.

The nature of disruptive or revolutionary change

The dot.com boom gave the gurus the chance to talk about a new economic paradigm; the credit crunch has given the same gurus the chance to talk about another new economic paradigm, ranging from the end of capitalism to new capitalism. From boom to bust, the hype may change but it never goes away. Booms and busts are episodic: they may be dramatic, but once they are over normal service will resume. Revolutionary change is not about the business cycle. It is about structural change. Structural change is happening at two levels:

- At an industry level: whole markets are changing
- Within a firm: the nature of management and power is changing

For a moment, we will focus on industry level disruptive change. Disruptive change involves asymmetric competition. Established firms in established industries fight a symmetrical battle: Hertz versus Avis, P&G versus Unilever; Deloitte versus PwC; one bank against another. The competition is intense, but the competitors follow broadly the same rules. Success is partly a matter of legacy (who has inherited the best market position and greatest scale) and partly it is down to operational excellence and incremental improvements and changes. In practice, all the competitors are improving and innovating incrementally. Any profit improvement promised by an internal improvement is typically competed away in the marketplace. All the competitors run harder every year, but remain stationary relative to each other.

Asymmetric competition comes about when a competitor changes the rules of the game. This is about business models, not technology. Incumbents, even market leaders, find it very hard to compete against a new business model.

For example, SouthWest Airlines and Ryanair did not invent new technology to attack traditional carriers. They created a new business model. To hear Michael O'Leary talk about Ryanair's competitive strategy versus BA is a model of simplicity and bravado. Here is his comparison of BA and Ryanair's sources of competitive advantage:

BA's advantages	Ryanair's advantages
Heathrow landing slots	Low cost
Global network	Low cost
Airline alliances	Low cost
Loyalty programmes	Low cost
In-flight catering and video	Low cost
Business class lounges	Low cost
Corporate sales network	Low cost

Ryanair's low cost focus creates space where BA cannot compete. Ryanair has one type of aircraft; they fly from secondary airports with low costs and quick turnaround times; their customer complaints department appears to be a garbage bin; they charge for every nonessential from manual check-in and checked bags to, possibly, use of the toilet in-flight. In 2002 Ryanair had operating costs of 5 US cents per seat kilometre versus 12 US cents per seat kilometre for BA. And BA was efficient relative to other European carriers. There is simply no way that BA's business model can match the costs of Ryanair's business model. BA can sell some economy seats at marginal cost in an attempt to compete on price, but otherwise Ryanair will always win on cost and price. This allows it to tap new demand. In the year to February 2009, Ryanair carried 58.4 million passengers, BA carried 35.7 million passengers. Ryanair's success has not come at the expense of BA, which carries more passengers than 10 years ago. Success has come by creating new market space.

Asymmetric warfare is not always so benign. When Canon entered the copier market it had none of the advantages of Xerox which dominated the market. In many cases, customers were tied to Xerox through long operational leases of the high end copiers which Xerox produced, financed and maintained for customers. With customers tied in, competitors appeared locked out. Canon thought otherwise. They did not fight Xerox on its own turf. Instead, they created a line of low end copiers. They created a new business model:

Xerox copier business model	Canon copier business model
Lease, through direct sales force	Buy from retailer
Fast, centralised copying	Slow, distributed copying
High maintenance, high service	Easy to maintain or replace
Used by central copy department	Used by secretaries
Expensive	Cheap

There was no reason for Xerox to compete: they did not have the infrastructure to serve the market which Canon was creating and did not want to cannibalise their own business. They had to focus on optimising their own business model: creating better machines, improving reliability and service and maximising profitability through incremental improvement.

At first, Canon was creating new market space. Xerox was not being harmed so it felt no need to tackle the upstart which was serving a market segment they did not want or need to serve. But experience in the low end of the copier market gave Canon experience and know-how. It was slowly able to build up its capability and introduce better machines. Some of the better machines simply strengthened their position in the low end of the market. Others began to nibble at the edges of Xerox market. Eventually, Canon built the strength to take on Xerox in its home market: the high end of high speed volume copiers. Only at this stage was Xerox able to engage in meaningful battle with Canon.

Disruptive change may be technologically enabled, but technology alone is not enough. There always has to be a compelling business model for a disruptive change to succeed. Business history is littered with failures where the excellence of technology has not been mirrored by the excellence of the business model. A few examples will make the point:

- Clive Sinclair, a British inventor, developed the C5. It was an electric car which would revolutionise urban transport. It might have succeeded if anyone had been able to stop laughing when they saw the car: it was a single seat vehicle, open to the elements and was so low to the ground that it had to carry a flag at the back so that other road users could see it.
- The dot.com boom spawned businesses whose only success was measured in eyeball count: they reported profits as sales before costs. WebVan (grocery deliveries) and Boo.com (clothes retailing) were fundamentally misconceived business models which wiped out their shareholders. The success models are obvious to us now: Amazon, Skype, eBay, travel sites suit the web. Their success relative to other business models was not obvious at the start of the dot.com boom.
- Internet search engines compete not just on the basis of the excellence of the search engine, but on the strength of their business model. We now know that paid search is the way to make money (and this reinforces the position of the market

leader, Google). But it was not obvious when the internet started: AOL and many others tried subscription models and banner advertising models which were natural models imported from the pre-web world. They failed in web world.

In all of the examples we have seen so far, the disruptive change has been based on asymmetric competition. The asymmetric competition has come in one of three flavours:

- Creating new market space and new demand (Ryanair, discount airlines, eBay)
- Serving underserved market segments (Canon)
- Serving the existing market in a new way (Amazon books: wide selection, low prices and reader reviews of books, avoid the cost of physical retail space)

In each case, the challengers created a new business model which the incumbents could not copy, and often had no incentive to copy. Incumbents naturally focus on defending what they have and optimising profits from their existing customers, products and business model. Market leaders are often weaker than they look. They have money and power to beat off any direct challenge, but they are very vulnerable to a good new idea: the disruptive business model.

The nature of disruptive change means that it is very difficult to predict. No-one in the staid world of book retailing in 1995 would have guessed at the revolution that was about to engulf them as Amazon built its empire. Once again, this means that incumbents tend to stick with their tried and tested business models. They cannot see change coming, and most firms experience evolutionary change, not revolutionary change. There is simply nothing in their corporate experience which prepares them for disruptive change.

It is tempting, but probably wrong, to believe that disruptive change is down to the genius of the innovators. Very smart people have backed very flawed models: Webvan's CEO George Shaheen had previously been CEO of Accenture (then named Andersen Consulting). Jeff Bezos founded Amazon in 1994: Amazon has been a huge success but Bezos has found it difficult to replicate his Eureka moment with books in other markets. A few of the failed or failing initiatives from Amazon include:

- Amazon auctions, which has not made inroads into eBay
- Amazon/Sotheby's joint venture, which is now quietly forgotten
- Amazon's line of Pinzon private label goods
- zShops, which was an on-line fixed price marketplace

Few people can predict which disruptive changes will succeed. Market research and analysis are of limited use when you are attempting to create a new market or a new business model. The only way to succeed is by trying it: that takes courage and the flexibility to adapt quickly to marketplace reaction.

Disruptive change strongly favours new challengers over incumbents:

- Incumbents have no incentive to threaten their existing business model: they focus on serving existing markets better.
- Incumbents are trapped by past experience: they tend to predict the future as an extrapolation of the past.

- Incumbents do not have the experience to cope with disruptive change.
- Challengers can open up new markets, serve underserved market segments and succeed with a different economic and business model.

Eventually, the challengers become established players with established business models. They then become vulnerable to the next wave of upstarts who do things differently. The business revolution never stops: it simply shifts focus from one sector to another. Periods of creative destruction are short punctuation marks in long periods of equilibrium. The credit crunch has led to upheaval in the banking world: give it five years and the industry will settle down to a new equilibrium. By then, another industry will be in upheaval. The nature of disruptive changes means we cannot tell where the next upheaval will be. For incumbents, this is an unsettling proposition: you cannot tell when you will face disruptive competition and you are not going to be able to cope with it. For entrepreneurs who are prepared to innovate and take risk, this is an exciting opportunity.

Why firms struggle with evolutionary change

To put the challenge of revolutionary change into perspective, it is worth looking at how firms struggle even with evolutionary change. Firms which struggle with evolutionary change are unlikely to succeed with revolutionary change.

Although change is difficult, firms need to change for both external and internal reasons. The external case for change is obvious: there is a constant need to improve to meet increasing customer needs and increasing competitive threats. The internal case for change is subtler but equally strong. Most firms are like sharks: they cannot stand still. Growth may be challenging, but it maintains morale. Curiously, crises and cut backs can also be managed: they create a sense of direction and purpose. When there is no movement neither forwards nor backwards, morale tends to plummet, politics rise and people create work for each other. The organisation quietly starts to implode.

For the last 20 years, one tool has consistently identified the ability of organisations to change successfully or not at all. It is called the change equation: use it on your own firm and decide how far your firm is ready to make real change. Here it is in all its spurious mathematical accuracy:

$$N \times V \times C \times F > R$$

Where:

N = Need for change
V = Vision of the end goal and benefits
C = Capacity to change
F = First steps
R = Risks and costs of change.

What it means is that the need, vision, capacity and first steps of change have to be stronger and greater than the perceived costs and risks of change. As with all simplistic formulas, it must be used with caution. If it is treated as a magic formula which solves the challenge of change, then it belongs in the dustbin of modern management. If it is used as a starting point for intelligent enquiry, then it can help generate insight around why many change initiatives fail. To understand how this formula works in practice we need to understand each piece of the formula.

Need for change

If there is no pain, there is no perceived need to change. Pain is both firm wide change and personal pain. Clearly, if the firm is losing market share there is pain for the firm. But if people in technical research or accounting or elsewhere do not feel the effects of losing market share, they are unlikely to feel any great need to change things. When there is a risk of losing jobs, reduced bonus and promotion opportunities, then the pain becomes personal and change is taken seriously. If there is little pain for the firm or individual, then change may start, inspired by a great vision, but it will then quickly stop at the first sign of trouble.

Vision of the end goal and benefits

CEOs often wax lyrical about how they will transform the organisation. There are several problems with this. First, most staff will ask "What's in it for me?" Improving earnings per share may help the CEO get a bigger bonus, but probably involves more work, higher targets and more stress for individual staff members. CEOs often sell visions which they love and staff hate. Second, despite the rhetoric, many firms are abysmal at identifying, tracking and following through on the targeted benefits of change, which are usually subject to much game playing. One consulting firm decided that 50% of its business had to come from e-commerce projects. Immediately every partner simply reclassified existing work as e-commerce: target met, nothing changed. Even where change does improve things, any benefits tend to be competed away: competitors are improving roughly as fast and any benefits accrue to customers, not shareholders.

Capacity for change

There can be deep cynicism in many firms about change: another year, another CEO and another crackpot change initiative. Keep your head down and it will all blow over. A firm's capacity to change is shaped by the credibility of management. If management have a history of half baked change, then each initiative will be met with increased cynicism. Successful change requires strong political support from the top: only they can put together the best team for the change, and give it the time, resources, direction and support required to succeed.

First steps

Everyone likes to back a winner. When it comes to change, most people are happy to stand on the sidelines and see how things go. If things start poorly, a chorus of negativity starts up with the line "I told you so …", If things start well, people quietly jump on board the bandwagon and opposition lifts like early morning mist on a sunny day. This often means seeking out some early, symbolic wins to show that this time change is serious and it will work. If change is seen as inevitable, people will go along with it. Give people the chance to doubt and question, and they will need no second invitation.

Risks and costs of change

There are obviously costs and risks of change for the firm. Because they are obvious, they are dealt with. More dangerous are the personal risks and costs of change: change is not rational. It is deeply political, emotional and personal. Unless the personal, emotional and political aspects of change are dealt with, change will be killed off. There will be a tsunami of apparently rational objections to the change, which are cover for personal objections to change.

Change means that individuals have to change: they may get a new boss, have to learn new skills, meet new targets. All of that means risk and hard work for uncertain reward. Overcoming this requires a critical mass of supporters of change who have to be flattered, cajoled and threatened to get behind the programme. Once there is a critical mass, the rest of the organisation will either follow or will at least mute their resistance to change.

Reflect on your own firm's attempts at making change. If it struggles, the chances are that at least some of the preconditions for change mentioned above are not in place. And if your firm struggles with evolutionary change, do not expect it to succeed in the face of revolutionary change.

Making change work

If managers want change to make a difference then they have to make sure that the preconditions for successful change are in place. The change equation gives a good first start at estimating whether the firm is ready to change. It also indicates what more needs to be done to set the change up for success. Critically, there has to be a sufficiently powerful coalition in support of change. Creating the alliances to make change happen is a time consuming politics, which many naïve project managers simply ignore. Once again, political skills rear their ugly head: they are essential for the success of the firm as well as for the success of the individual. It is a skill set which is often in short supply: there are many project managers but few effective change leaders.

To make change work, managers have to go beyond the simplicity of a formula like the change equation. Change that really makes a difference tends to have three further characteristics:

(a) It raises levels of ambition even further
(b) It makes change a whole firm effort
(c) Results are measured

Raise levels of ambition even further: from best practice to next practice
Many managers are already working hard, and they work harder each year. But even though they run harder and faster each year, they make no progress against the competition, who are also running harder and faster each year. Projected profit improvements turn out to be mirages. They disappear in the heat of marketplace competition. This is the fallacy of the stable baseline: improvement efforts are measured against a stable baseline, which may be this year's performance. In practice, the baseline is not stable. It is always declining. Internally, the forces of entropy and chaos are at work: new staff join, experienced staff leave; suppliers mess up; forecasts go awry and cock ups happen. Externally, market forces are at work: competitors innovate, reduce prices, poach customers. A huge amount of effort and improvement is required simply to match this year's performance. To improve, managers need to raise their levels of ambition even further.

Many change programmes aim to make a company best in class, or have best benchmark costs, or achieve best practice. These are worthy goals, but implicitly they are follower strategies. Consultants are guilty of encouraging the follower strategy. They will never directly sell your secrets to a rival. Instead, they will package up some "anonymous" cases on best practice and sell that best practice to you. By the time you reach the best practice benchmark, plus or minus a bit, the leader you are copying will have moved on. You will still be behind, and the consultants will be ready to sell you the next best practice programme.

To make a difference, change has to aim not at best practice, but at next practice. Next practice means getting off the better-fastercheaper treadmill. It requires rethinking how you will serve the market. Re-engineering, originally, was not just about cost cutting: it started by thinking through how to serve the market better. Done well, it leads to solutions which are radical and effective. For instance, the simplest piece of re-engineering was inadvertently created by Michael Dell when he started his PC business on a shoestring budget. Because he had minimal capital he could not build computers and then hope to sell them. He had to sell the computers and then hope to build them. So the value chain for traditional PC makers and Dell looked like this, in simplified form:

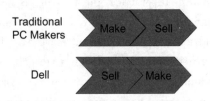

With that one radical move, Dell got rid of all the problems of forecasting, stock outs when a line was too popular, fire sales to move unpopular lines and the costs of building and managing a network of resellers. By 1999 Dell had inventory of six days against an industry average of 65 days and an inventory turn of 60 times versus 10–14 times for traditional firms. Other firms were still implementing change programmes aimed at improving forecasting, reducing cycle times to minimise stock problems, and minimising inventory. However hard they worked, they could not match Dell on inventory and working capital with their old model. They were all focused on best practice. Dell created next practice.

Change should not be about working harder. It should be about working smarter.

Make change a whole firm effort

Achieving next practice is a whole firm effort. Dell's approach to the PC business changed the way every part of the firm worked. If a firm wants to increase speed to market, no one department can achieve that goal: marketing, manufacturing, logistics, design, purchasing and all the other departments have to collaborate on that one goal. Achieving this level of collaboration is like herding cats. The technical problems of managing change pale into insignificance compared to the political challenges of getting alignment across the firm around priorities.

Many change programmes disappear down into a black hole of politics and internal competition. At its worst, change disintegrates into a series of risk logs, issue logs, meeting logs, telephone logs, attendance logs, progress logs and master logs. This is the land of the project manager proudly displaying his PRINCE2 qualification and mastery of its 45 separate subprocesses. Technical project management is important, but can only succeed in the context of successful change management: that requires focus on the right goal and aligning the politics behind the right goal.

At this point it is enough to note that success or failure is often determined before the programme formally starts. Success depends on creating an alliance of the right people in support of change: each person needs to see that they can win from the change and that they retain some control over their destiny. Creating an alliance like this takes a huge amount of time and effort.

Where change happens on an ad hoc basis within departments, any gains seem to be illusory. Improvement in one department is worthy, but often has no visible effect on firm wide improvement. On a grand scale this happened with the UK government. In 2004–5 the Gershon report found that the public sector could achieve £21.5 billion of efficiency gains out of a budget of £492 billion: that is a relatively modest 5% productivity gain. Three years later, the civil service declared that the goal had been achieved. Meanwhile, expenditure had risen 10% faster than inflation to £586 billion. There may have been efficiency gains or not: to the taxpayer they have become submerged by policy decisions to grow spending with the aim of improving services.

Measure the improvement

This is so obvious it should not need to be said. It needs to be said because many change efforts are not measured. Even when they start with big promises about the improvements which will result, management often lack the discipline to follow through. There are several reasons for this:

- Change is strategic: this is an excuse used to justify many large IT projects. "Strategic" is code for spending a lot of money without any payback. Given that senior executives often lack experience to challenge IT proposals and to look at alternatives, it is a sale which works remarkably well.
- Change is an enabler: HR and skills initiatives often fall into this category. No-one wants to argue against such worthy goals. But they raise the question: what, precisely, are these initiatives enabling?
- Change cannot be measured: even if the change succeeds, other factors such as market competition will make it impossible to read the results.

These objections melt away if the change is a whole firm effort focused on a clear goal. Goals can be non financial: quality, customer retention and speed to market are all potentially winning goals, and all of these are measurable goals. A goal which cannot be measured is of little use: even non financial goals should normally be measurable. If you are clear about the goals, you are in a much better position to decide if the IT project is genuinely strategic or if the HR initiatives are genuinely enabling the goal to be achieved.

The Western tradition is to go for the formal change programme which delivers a spectacular result: 20% cost reduction and promotions for the executives who led the effort. Once the 20% cost reduction is in the bag, the next change may look at a halving time to market, then the next might focus on a dramatic increase in quality. These campaigns are highly visible and highly effective, in the short term. The alternative is less visible but more effective. Instead of having a series of campaigns, Japanese firms make change a way of life. Improving by 5% a year is better than a 20% improvement once every four years. By making change part of the fabric of the firm, it is far more sustainable than the one-off 18-month campaigns beloved of senior management and consultants.

How managers cope with change

By now, hopefully, we have established that change is not just rational. It is about people and politics, not just projects. And most people feel ambivalent about change. They know that it is good in theory, but they would prefer it if change happened to other people, thank you very much. Change involves too much personal risk, hard work and stress. Changing the firm is good, changing yourself is threatening. Personal change implies learning new skills, adapting to a new boss, delivering new performance outcomes. It means leaving behind a tried and trusted success formula and replacing it with something that is neither tried nor tested. At a rational level, change is good. At an emotional and personal level change is not so good.

Managers' ambivalence to change has adverse consequences for themselves and for the firm.

Firms find most change programmes meet stiff resistance, and the resistance comes from the enemy within: management resist management change. The resistance to change is invariably dressed up in rational terms based on risk, cost, lost opportunities, time and effort, the need for further testing and analysis. Some of these challenges are legitimate. But in many cases they are smokescreens for personal and political resistance to change. Change upsets the political order within a company and threatens individual managers. These are not legitimate grounds for objection, so managers hide their concerns behind some rational objections to change.

Mixing rational, emotional and political objections to change leads to chaos. Change champions will struggle valiantly to overcome the rational objections to change, which plays straight into the hands of the objectors to change: they can erect rational hurdles to change faster than the change champions can dismantle them. The change champions will never win this game if they play it rationally. They can only win if they go for the political power play: "the CEO requires this ..." will gain grudging compliance, if not commitment. Alternatively, the change champions have to deal with the unstated emotional fears and concerns of the objectors. They have to show that the future will not be as risky and as threatening as feared, and will be less risky than staying in the existing comfort zone. Fighting emotional objections with rational arguments is like fighting fire with fuel.

Typically, the main resistance comes from the middle of the organisation: there is a layer of concrete which does not want to change. Executives at the top are more in control of change and can shape their own destiny: they have less to fear. At the bottom of the organisation, there is often frustration with the status quo and people are happy to see things change: the new is likely to be better than the old. Also, junior levels are often populated by younger people who have not yet become set in their ways. For managers in the middle, the prospect of change is not appealing. They do not have control over their own destiny; they have much to lose personally in terms of position and power and it is not clear what they will gain.

The risk aversion of middle managers may be influenced by their career prospects. Older employees typically have the longest tenure in the firm and they also have the lowest prospects of being employed elsewhere. The employment participation rate for males aged 55–64 in the USA in 2005 was just 44%, versus 75% for all males aged 20–64. This makes older employees more loyal and more risk averse: anything which threatens their job security is unwelcome. Change is rarely seen to enhance job security.

Change resistance from managers makes even evolutionary change very hard. Revolutionary or disruptive change becomes more or less impossible. Managers fear that they will not have the skills for the new world; in-built risk aversion means they also lack the will to push for revolutionary change when it is required. Organisations, like managers, are relatively conservative: they prefer to improve incrementally on their existing success formula than risk trying something completely new. This is a mindset which is completely acceptable in a world which is changing incrementally: there is no need to take great risk. When the competitive landscape faces disruptive change, legacy managers and organisations are poorly equipped to keep pace with the change required.

Change resistance is not just for the marzipan layer of middle managers. Successful managers can be even more resistant. They may be willing to embrace modest corporate change, but they are less willing to embrace personal change. By definition, a successful manager is someone who has a success formula: they have figured out what works and what does not work in their situation. The longer they have been successful, the more entrenched that success formula becomes in their mindset, behaviour and habits. Change challenges that success formula by creating a new set of conditions in which the manager has to work.

By the time a successful manager reaches the executive suite, they have perfected their success formula. A cost cutter remains at heart a cost cutter; someone who built their reputation by building new markets remains committed to that model of success. Appointing the CEO should be done with this in mind: it is less important to find the "ideal" CEO. It is more important to understand the challenges that face the firm, and then appoint a CEO whose success model fits that challenge.

Conclusions

Success is the enemy of change. The more successful a firm or a manager becomes, the less they want to change their success formula. This is natural and rational, but it makes change hard to achieve. The greater the change, the greater the resistance.

Revolutionary change is hardest of all: when faced with a new entrant competing in a different way, incumbent firms simply work harder to protect what they have. This helps explain why the half life of most top firms is between 20 and 25 years. When the world changes around them, they cannot change fast enough or far enough.

Even evolutionary change is hard. Simply fighting the forces of entropy and maintaining order is hard enough. Making any improvement is harder: as fast as a firm improves, so do its competitors. Improvements do not feed through to better market share of improved profits: the improvements are competed away and the main beneficiaries are customers, not shareholders. In any firm, any change faces huge obstacles.

Within the firm, change faces huge obstacles. Change is not a purely rational process about project management. It is an intensely political and personal process which requires building alliances, overcoming resistance, begging resources and building momentum for change. This is at the heart of the management job, and yet most managers feel ambivalent about change. They know it is right in theory but they also know that it can be painful personally. Successful change leaders are not just project managers: they go beyond rational management and manage the personal and political aspects of change as well.

We started with Darwin, and we will finish with Hamlet 5.2: "There's a divinity that shapes our ends, rough hew them how we may." Most change is about rough hewing the destiny of the firm, rather than fundamentally changing it. Leopards don't change their spots, dinosaurs don't dance and most firms do not radically change direction. Success lasts as long as the world does not change too dramatically – in the new world disorder, we may need to get used to seeing more change and shorter-lived success.

Chapter Nine

Employees: From Slavery to Freedom (and Back Again)

Twenty-five years ago, one of the top executives at P&G turned up to a conference wearing grey socks. It was the start of a sartorial revolution. The conformity of black socks and the corporate uniform was being challenged. Twenty-five years later, at a Skype conference in Estonia, the only person not wearing a T-shirt was a guest speaker. Even the CEO was in a T-shirt and jeans. In between the suit and T-shirt there is a bewildering array of dress codes for different functions, in different organisations at different times.

Conformity and certainty is being replaced by diversity and ambiguity. We cannot even be sure of a desk to work at: much derided cubicle land is becoming a fond memory among people who now fight to get in early to find a place to hot desk.

As employees, the management revolution pulls us in opposite directions. We are promised much tomorrow, but even more is demanded from us today. We are caught between the forces of freedom and slavery.

Five forces drive the revolution as employees experience it:

1. Technology allows us to be more productive and makes difficult tasks easier. But this has not made life easier for employees: it has made it harder. Technology has not reduced workloads. It has raised expectations. Where a 10-page presentation with one or two charts would have been acceptable before, now we all suffer from death by PowerPoint. Quantity has increased, even if the quality has not. We are not being freed by technology, we are being enslaved by it.

2. Work has become more ambiguous. Working on a production line or in a call centre it is very obvious how much work each person has done. They can feel like sweat shops where every ounce of productivity is squeezed out of each team member. But more and more work is shifting to the world of professional services and office workers in cubicle land. It is much harder to measure the productivity of a lawyer, consultant, accountant or civil servant. We can measure how long they work and how much they bill, but that is different from knowing how productive they are. While some staff take the opportunity to hide and shirk, most employees find that they work harder than ever to fulfil expectations which are often highly ambiguous.

3. Work–life balance is disappearing. The days when people worked from 9 to 5 are going. This is not just about the rise of flexitime. It is also about the demise of compartmentalisation. In the past, work life and home life were different worlds. Now technology means that work and home life are co-mingled. We may do emails from home, but book our holiday on the web while at work. In theory, this is liberating. In practice it seems

to lead to more stress. We never fully free ourselves from the shackles of work.

4. Employers are imposing the tyranny of freedom on staff. The days of the paternalistic employer are long gone: few people outside the public sector expect to stay with one employer all their lives. The one company town, corporate welfare and final salary pensions are becoming distant memories. Employees now have to look after themselves.

5. Loyalty has become a one way street. Employers expect passion and commitment, if their values statements are to be believed. In return, they offer a job until the next downsizing, re-engineering, restructuring, outsourcing or best shoring exercise swings through town. Staff know that employment is insecure. Security comes from employability, not employers. To survive, we have to invest in our own skills and to keep pace with the changing demands of the marketplace. Employability gives us freedom and insecurity at the same time.

The question is how we, as employees, can survive and succeed in this new world. The old psychological contract between employer and employee is over. Most of us cannot expect a job for life, and many of us do not want to be tied to one employer for ever. If we let our employer control our destiny, we become slaves who are likely to be cast aside at the whim of the employer. We have to control our own destiny if we want to taste the benefits of freedom, not slavery.

Controlling our destiny has four elements:

1. Become employable, not just an employee
2. Compartmentalise your life

3. Avoid the hedonic trap
4. Build your resilience

Become employable, not just an employee

Organisations have only a limited interest in developing their staff. There is little point in preparing everyone for promotion when only a few people can be promoted. In practice, organisations need people to take on ever more specialised tasks. As organisations grow, as value chains fragment, so each individual task becomes ever more specialised. And organisations are very happy for you to develop such specialised skills. Once you have those skills, they have little incentive to teach the dog new tricks. If you get promoted or move job, it costs time and money to train up your replacement. It is easier to let people remain in post with their specialised skills.

The trend towards specialisation is unstoppable in most industries. From Adam Smith and pins, specialisation is extending deep into the knowledge industries and professional services. University PhD theses are now celebrations of obscurity. Professionals find themselves specialised in ever smaller parts of the law, consulting or IT. Building deep expertise is necessary, but dangerous in terms of employability. Being a specialist is like being a niche business: when demand is good, then life is very good. COBOL programmers made a good living when there were not enough of them. When demand dropped and supply from India shot up, COBOL programmers became as fashionable as purple flared trousers, brown cheese cloth shirts and green crushed velvet jackets, worn together. A speciality can go out of fashion very fast.

Relying on your employer for your career may have been essential 100 years ago, desirable 50 years ago and possible 20 years ago. It is no longer possible for most people. Instead of relying on your employer, you have to rely on yourself. You are freed from the tyranny of your employer: the freedom of the market can be even more tyrannical unless you can tame it.

"Become employable" is easier to say than to do. Towns which used to rely on coal and steel are still unemployment hot spots. Becoming employable depends on building the right skills and then finding the right employer for those skills. Having such job mobility depends on the whole family accepting mobility: the right employer may not be in your existing community. Two considerations drive "the right skills" part of the employability formula:

- preferences
- experience

First, focus on your strengths. This is blindingly obvious, which is why most assessment systems miss the point. Annual assessments often find areas for staff to remediate and improve: the idea is that if you improve those weaknesses, you will become a better employee. No-one succeeded by focusing on their weaknesses. Do not ask an Olympic weightlifter to compete in synchronised swimming: they may amuse, but they will not win. The reality is that we all have weaknesses. But fortunately, management is increasingly a team sport. That is the essence of the knowledge economy: creating a network of deep specialist skills which works together. So if we are weak at project management, or accounting, or strategic analysis, there are plenty of other people who can do it for us. Focus on what you are good at, and work with a team who fill in for your blind spots. Do not run by focusing on your blind spots: you will only get a bloody nose.

Second, experience drives the sort of skills we need. When we start out our career, or if we decide to change career, we find we have to spend up to five years learning the craft skills of our new trade: accounting, law, engineering, plumbing and selling all require mastery of some core technical skills. But these technical skills can be a barrier to advancement. Once we have mastered those skills, we find that we have to start acquiring new skills if we want promotion. Managers are no longer players. Few top sports stars become great managers; most great sports coaches were journeymen players. Playing and managing are fundamentally different skills.

A soccer player has to run, tackle, pass, shoot and argue with the referee. The soccer manager waves his arms in disgust at the side of the pitch and argues with the referee's assistant; he also has to pick the right team, decide the tactics, set the direction, motivate the team, train them and coach them. If the manager started running on to the pitch to tackle an opposition player, all hell would break loose and he would probably miss the tackle anyway.

The difference between playing and managing may be obvious in the sports world, but it is routinely missed in the business world. Promotion systems work on the basis that only the best players can be promoted to the management ranks. Aspiring managers make the same mistake: they hope that by being the best player they will become a great manager. When they are promoted, they then work harder and better than ever before. Then they get fired, because they have not been managing well. They have been trying to make all the tackles and shoot all the goals instead of coaching and building the team.

Technical and craft skills become less important as careers advance. Instead, people and political skills become far more important. The nature of these skills will be explored further in the section on Management. At this stage, all that is required is to note the change from being a player to a manager. The job of the manager is to make things happen through other people. Managers do not have control over all the people they need to influence: this is what makes people and political skills essential for survival. Many great team players get promoted and fail because they do not understand how to make the transition from playing to managing.

Compartmentalise your life

In days long gone, work was work and home was home. If people took a briefcase to and from work it was more likely to carry sandwiches and a crossword than real work. Once you left the office, you left work. Nowadays, we are always on and we believe that we are working 24/7. In truth, the old days were not golden, and today is not as tough as our propaganda makes out.

The old world of 9 to 5 gave a clear distinction between work and leisure. Life was led at a more relaxed pace. Everything was slower, from transport to advertising. At the height of the postal era, between the two world wars, someone could send a letter across town in the morning and might just get a reply in the evening. Now we expect a reply to our emails across the globe within the hour, and hope for it within a few minutes. But if there was a golden age, it was a golden prison for many women who found that their place was at home washing and cooking for the family. If the wife depended on the husband, the husband depended on the employer. If you had ambition and wanted freedom, it was hell. If you were prepared to sign up to the corporate life, it was a cosy prison for all.

The new world has torn down the barriers between home and work. Technology allows us to work anywhere. The result is that we think we are working all the time. This is not true. A few indicators show that actual working time is probably going down, not going up:

- Watch rush hour: have you really experienced a bad crush on the 7.45 am train on Sunday morning?
- Try fixing a meeting for after 5.30 pm.
- Track your email traffic: typically 85% comes between 8.30 am and 6 pm Monday to Friday.
- Track usage of your company website: as with email, about 85% of visitors will arrive between 8.30 am and 6 pm Monday to Friday.
- Average working hours per year have declined from around 3200 hours a year in 1850 to 1820 hours 150 years later in the UK: even the hardest working group (senior managers) claim to work an average of just 46.3 hours a week. That is idle compared to the standards of the Industrial Revolution.

These indicators show that we are not meeting, emailing or even in the office for 100-hour weeks. Of course, if the EU Working Time Directive was really enforced, and all employees were required to work 35 hours a week, disaster would ensue. In many organisations, employees would find themselves having to spend at least 100 hours a week in the office to achieve 35 hours of meaningful work, once you ignore Facebook time, gossip time, idling time, coffee time and inefficient working and meeting time. Presumably, that is not what the EU regulators had in mind with the Working Time Directive.

Even if the reality is that we are not working much harder than previous generations, our perceptions are that workloads have increased dramatically. Perceptions may not be real, but the consequences of perceptions are real. We now feel more stressed and more harassed than ever before. We may leave the office, but the office never leaves us. We are shackled to work by the fetters of email, internet and all the other technology that was meant to improve our lives. We have to learn to control our technology before it controls us.

Core to learning to control technology is finding the 'off' switch. The 'off' switch cannot be found on the technology: even if we turn off our computer and phone it is still 'on' in our heads: we still think guiltily about what messages we are missing, who we need to contact and what we need to be doing. The only real 'off' switch is in our heads.

We have not yet discovered how to master the 'off' switch or to control technology. We invest billions in developing ever more sophisticated software, but virtually nothing into understanding how we can live with technology, as opposed to becoming more productive with it. The current state of the art is little more than a series of tricks which people use to cope:

- Go cold turkey: turn off email and phones completely, leaving messages saying you will be out of the office until … In theory this works well. In practice it comes up against the prejudices of co-workers and bosses who want you to suffer as much as they do: being on call 24/7 is a way of showing corporate commitment.

- Soft withdrawal: set aside times each day when you will catch
  up with work. Even if this means doing 15 minutes last thing at
  night (and giving co-workers the impression you have been
  working non stop), that can allow you time off for other important things like family, eating and television.
- Delegate better: use team members, co-workers, secretarial staff
  to pick up the slack in your absence. The executive sitting on
  the beach with a blackberry is not just paranoid: he is also
  showing an inability to delegate and an arrogance which comes
  from thinking he is the only person capable of dealing with all
  the day to day crises of corporate life.
- Know what is important: most of the daily routine involves
  trivia. By focusing on the two or three things that will really
  make a difference over the week, month or year it becomes
  possible to cancel out most of the corporate noise and interfer-
  ence. Unimportant stuff can either be dealt with later or, if it is
  urgent trivia such as agreeing a meeting time, it can be dele-
  gated to support staff.

The purpose of all these tricks is to regain control over our most
precious resource: time. If we can stop work polluting our private
life, we regain control and reduce the perceived stress of our daily
lives.

Avoid the hedonic trap

Employers have always been happy to have employees who are
completely dependent on them. Just as dogs learn loyalty to the

person who feeds them, so employees learned loyalty to the employer who paid them. In the past, dependence could be absolute: pay, pensions, health care, education and housing all depended on the employer.

Rising affluence should have made us more independent of our employers. It has not. The simplest way to ensure dependence is to overpay staff. This is routinely done in professional services firms, from banking to consulting. For example, one consulting company will hire engineers earning £40 000 a year. It will train them for one month, and then start billing them out to clients at £240 000 a year. The engineer will now be earning £60 000 a year. A 50% pay increase, with the prospect of more to come, sounds wonderful. The engineer's family quickly gets used to the £60 000 a year lifestyle. Returning to the days of getting by on just £40 000 would involve unbearable sacrifices. Suddenly, the engineer is trapped on a treadmill: unfortunately, the employer controls the speed of the treadmill, and wants as much out of each person as possible.

It is possible for the overpaid employee to switch employers. In practice, they are not looking for a slower treadmill with less pay: they nearly always want a faster treadmill with more pay.

This is the hedonic trap: we find it easy to adapt to more income, but very hard to adapt to less.

There are two ways of escaping the hedonic trap. One way is to make so much money so fast that you no longer rely on an employer; you can choose what you want to do. This is the dream of many workers in financial services: slave away for 15 years and then retire to fulfil some long held day dream. This theory works spectacularly well for a few, but for the majority is a pipe dream which fails for three reasons:

(a) Success proves elusive. The super rich winners grab all the headlines. The losers vastly outnumber the winners but are quietly ignored.

(b) Expectations rise faster than reality. Even the successful players find that the more they earn the more they need. Money is less a matter of putting bread on the table: it is a matter of keeping score and proving your self worth against your peers. That means you need to earn more than them. For these people, success requires running faster than anyone else on the treadmill, which is fine for people who enjoy running fast on treadmills.

(c) Success is an empty vessel. A simple exercise I do with staff is to ask them what they would do if they won the lottery jackpot. Think about this yourself. Here are the normal answers:
- Go on holiday
- Pay off the mortgage
- Go on holiday again
- Buy a big car
- Go on holiday yet again
- Buy another car
- And then …?

Most people land up realising they would go back to work: normally a different sort of work, but it would still be work. It is at this point people discover the alternative way of escaping the hedonic trap. Instead of making countless millions of dollars, discover what you really want to do. If working 24/7 is what turns you on, fine. If working in the community is the thing for you, do it.

In the years leading to the credit crunch, self worth was based on net worth. The better off were better than the rest. Social vocations, such as teaching, were perceived as being for losers: "if you can't do, teach" summed up the dismissive attitude to teaching. That is now changing. In the UK, Teach First has become one of the top 10 graduate recruiters nationally, and at top universities such as Oxford and Cambridge. Teach First places teachers in the most challenging inner city schools, where the workload and the stress is at least as great as in consulting, law, accounting or banking. Personal success and fulfilment is no longer purely about net worth: it can also be about experience and value.

When we realise we have choices about the nature of success, and when we exercise those choices, we can rediscover freedom.

Build your resilience

Career is both a noun and a verb: some people have a career, other people career through life. "Career" used to be a noun which described how people slowly climbed the greasy pole of promotion at one employer, before they finally retired with a replica carriage clock. For many people, career is becoming a verb which describes the random walk of experience from one employer to another. Sometimes the movement is voluntary; often it is involuntary.

Average tenure in one company is declining. In the UK and the USA average tenure is 7.2 years and 7.6 years respectively. In more traditional economies and societies with greater employment protection, job tenure is typically 11–13 years (Japan, France, Germany and Italy). This mean average disguises considerable turmoil. Newer employees and younger employees are much more likely to move around. Data from the CIPD shows that 80% of employee turnover is concentrated among people who have been with the firm less than five years.

In the real world, this data makes sense. When people leave university they often do not really know what they want, despite the elegant stories they spin at recruiting interviews. They also do not really know what to expect in different sorts of organisation. If you do not know what you want or what you are going to get, then you will almost certainly be surprised by what you find. Some people get lucky and find a pleasant surprise. Other people decide to find another job.

Early years career hopping is now widely accepted. And everyone has a chance to play that ultimate career joker: the MBA. An MBA offers a limited amount of knowledge and an unlimited opportunity to reshape your career. The MBA is a very expensive dating service between students and employers.

The major shift has come with people in the first stages of their careers. The process of hopping between jobs for a few years is useful, for two reasons:

- Job hopping helps people discover the context where they are most likely to succeed. They do not depend on a single throw of the dice when they leave university. You only excel at what you enjoy. If you do not enjoy work, you will not want to put in all that extra discretionary effort from which you learn and which sets you apart from others. You will not have the stamina to last the career marathon.

- Job hopping builds resilience. Falling flat on your face and then finding another job removes fear and builds confidence. In contrast, people who have served their time for 20 years become very vulnerable. If they are suddenly let go in their mid forties, having only experienced one employer, they can be crushed. They lack the experience and capability to shift jobs easily, and much of their personal identity has become entwined with that of their employer.

Conclusions

The old Greek curse "may all your wishes be granted" has been laid on employees in the management revolution. Employees wanted to throw off the yoke of conformity imposed by paternalistic employers. That wish has been granted. Now we have acquired freedom, we are discovering the responsibility, anxiety and stress that goes with it. We have to rely on ourselves, not our employer, to be employable, to provide for our pensions and to manage our career.

At the same time as tasting freedom, we have discovered technology. Technology should have freed us, but it has imprisoned us in a world where, in our minds at least, we never escape from work. Freedom and technology will enslave us until we learn to cope with this new world. It is up to us to create our own heaven or hell: we have the tools and we have the choice.

Chapter Ten

Managers: Power and Making Things Happen

Management has always been the poor relation of leadership. Leaders get all the glory, while managers are left with all the work of converting the grand vision into reality.

At first sight, managers appear to have been the prime victims of the revolution. They have been re-engineered, delayered and hollowed out. The certainties of the past have been replaced with the anxieties of the present. In most ways, the job of the manager has become much harder:

- There are fewer managers left since cost cutting and re-engineering wiped out whole layers of management.
- The work has become more complicated: managers no longer live in comfortable functional silos, but have to work across the organisation with people over whom they have no control.
- Managers have to work longer than ever before, because there are fewer of them and demands have risen. Workers get protection over working hours, managers do not.

- Management is no longer a job for life with a carriage clock and an index linked pension as a retirement present. Ambiguity and stress are standard.

If you look again, you will find that the bad news is also very good news for managers. The art of good management has become more important than ever before. Let's turn the revolution on its head and see why managers can be the big winners in the revolution:

- Fewer managers means no organisation fat, so each manager becomes relatively more important to the success of the organisation.
- More complicated work means that managers, who always were the glue of the organisation, become even more essential in making the complexity work.
- As the job market becomes more liquid, organisations become ever more anxious about not losing good managers.

All revolutions create winners and losers, and the management revolution is no exception. For managers, this revolution is a flight to quality. Poor managers become very easily dispensable. Good managers become indispensable.

To understand how far the job of management has changed, we will revisit our short, revisionist history of management. This time, we will view history from a different angle: the nature of management skills. We will find that managers now require a new set of skills which simply do not exist in the current management literature. As ever, practice is years ahead of the theory. Our history comes in three parts

- The Enlightenment and rational management: IQ skills
- The twentieth century: the rise of humanity and EQ skills
- The twenty-first century: back to the future and the rise of PQ skills

The heart of the revolution for managers is the need to acquire a whole new set of skills. We already need IQ and EQ skills. The changing nature of the workplace now means that political skills are becoming essential. These are not political skills in terms of successful career management, although those help. These political skills are about knowing how to make things happen in a world where managers' responsibilities routinely exceed their authority.

The Enlightenment and Industrial Revolution: the rise of rational management

The Enlightenment brought with it a belief in progress through reason and rational investigation. From physics to economics under Newton and Adam Smith, there was a quest for the universal rules which lay behind everything. As the Enlightenment gave way to the Industrial Revolution, it was no surprise to find that the same mindset was applied to the newly emerging discipline of industrial management. The apotheosis of rational management was reached under Frederick Taylor who published *Scientific Management* in 1911. He believed in observation and measurement which led to some revolutionary ideas. For instance, he noted that rest breaks did not interrupt productivity, but enhanced it. 10 minutes' rest would generate 50 minutes' good effort; working straight through led to a worse result. Taylor did not have the workers' interests at heart: he was simply trying to maximise output. His ideas were revolutionary: previously management had been a craft skill based on judgement and rules of thumb. Although his method was new, his style was not. He still believed in strong command and control and had little trust in the workers. Below is a flavour of his style:

> It is only through *enforced* standardization of methods, *enforced* adoption of the best implements and working conditions, and *enforced* cooperation that this faster work can be assured. And the duty of enforcing the adoption of standards and enforcing this cooperation rests with *management* alone.

This was the epitome of reason. Workers were no more than units of production and were more dispensable than machinery. Managers managed and workers worked: bosses had the brains and the workers had the hands.

Perhaps not surprisingly, rational management started to become a dirty word. It became associated with sweat shops and conflict between unions and management: management always wanting to increase work rates, unions wanting to protect their members' interests. Although the West fell out of love with rational management, Japan reinvented it with devastating consequences. The reinvention of rational management by the Japanese owed much to another American, Edward Deming. Deming was pretty much ignored in his own country until near the end of his life, by which time the damage had been done.

Deming is the high priest of the quality movement. Put crudely, Taylor worked on quantity, Deming worked on quality. Like Taylor, Deming was highly focused on analysing and understanding quality. Inspecting for quality meant high cost and rework: designing and building in quality from the start led to lower costs and higher profit. The idea that higher quality and lower costs went hand in hand was itself a revolutionary concept. In 1960, Deming was awarded the Order of the Sacred Treasure by the Japanese government for his work. He was more or less unknown in America at the time: with a booming economy and endless demand, there seemed little need for Deming's ideas in the West. By the 1980s that complacency had gone as the Japanese industrial onslaught became clear. Now quality is an obsession, in its different guises, across most manufacturing industries.

Like Taylor, Deming was obsessed with observation and statistics. In this sense he was still a child of the Enlightenment and in the tradition of rational management. However, he also recognised that workers had an important role to play in helping assure quality.

The legacy of Taylor, Deming and rational management lives with us to this day. Process intensive industries, from auto and chemical plants to burger restaurants and call centres, owe both their productivity and quality to the heritage of Taylor and Deming. As consumers, we benefit greatly from the cost and quality improvements they have delivered.

In the world of rational management, the qualities needed of a manager were about observation, measurement, analysis, relaying instructions clearly. These are, for the most part, intellectual skills. Good IQ was a key to management success. To this day, that assumption remains strong. Entry to most Business Schools still depends heavily on the GMAT, which is a form of intelligence test. The real brain boxes go to Harvard, the less able do a distance learning MBA in the evenings with an obscure business school with little brand name recognition. The median GMAT score for

Harvard, Wharton, Stanford, Sloan and Yale is 710–720, which puts them in the top 7% of all candidates, who have already self-selected for being among the brightest of their generation. There is still a very strong presumption that the leaders of the future are going to be brains on sticks. As we shall see, this is a dangerous assumption.

The twentieth century and the rise of humanity

Slowly people ceased being mere units of production and consumption. They became better educated, which meant they could do more but they also expected more. They began to have choice over where they worked: the days of the one company town were quickly disappearing. Social security gave an option to people who could not or would not work. Managers began to discover that their workers had hopes and fears just like themselves. In other words, we discovered that workers were human beings. This had devastating consequences for management.

At the same time as Taylor was working on *Scientific Management*, Freud and his disciple Jung were leading the way in trying to understand humans. How far they succeeded is a matter of debate. The world of work was not ready for dealing with dreams, the unconscious and repressed sexuality: there were enough challenges with getting the books to balance without entering the world of psychoanalysis. But even in those early days, there were a few pioneers who began to recognise that the workplace was more than just an economic entity: it is also a social entity. As early as 1920, E. L. Thorndike was using the term "social intelligence" to describe the art of managing other people.

Slowly, managers recognised that there was more to managing than command and control. To get the best out of people, you had to treat them like people. Managers learned the arts of influence and persuasion. Effective workplaces became based more on commitment than on compliance. Earning the commitment of employees is hard work, but is an investment which pays off handsomely.

Management theory started to catch up with the new reality which Thorndike had hinted at. Seventy-five years after Thorndike published his work, Daniel Goleman published *Emotional Intelligence*. If Taylor was the high priest of rational management, Goleman turned out to be the high priest of emotional management.

Goleman confirmed what many practising managers already knew: rational management is not enough for success. Successful managers need good EQ (emotional quotient) as well as IQ. The performance bar for managers had been raised. The essence of Daniel Goleman's world is a world away from Taylor's rational world. Goleman talks of four keys: self-awareness, self-management, social awareness and relationship management. These qualities are hard to define, measure or learn despite the efforts of the whole Emotional Intelligence industry which has emerged over the last decade.

The twenty-first century: back to the future

If good management is about having a high IQ and a high EQ, then something is wrong. Look around your own organisation and you may well find people who are both smart and nice, but they languish harmlessly in the backwaters of the organisation.

Meanwhile, people who are neither as nice nor as smart seem to levitate towards the top of the organisation, using nice smart people as their doormats on the road to the top. Clearly, something is missing: it is not enough to have a high IQ and EQ in order to succeed.

That "something missing" is called power.

Effective managers need IQ, EQ and PQ: political quotient. Power skills are becoming more important because the nature of the manager's job is changing. It is now normal for managers to find that their responsibilities exceed their authority. In the past, the art of management was getting things done through other people, whom the manager controlled. Now managers have to get things done through other people *whom they do not control.* The lack of control changes everything. New skills are required to make things happen when you lack formal authority. These skills include:

- Building networks of trust and influence
- Creating alliances to make things happen
- Dealing with conflict
- Shaping the organisation's agenda to meet your needs
- Dealing with organisational conflict and resistance
- Managing ambiguity and uncertainty
- Finding the right assignments and projects to work on
- Discovering the real rules of survival and success in your firm

These are familiar tasks for managers who find themselves fighting to get things done. They are not skills which are recognised IQ or EQ skills; they do not exist in training programmes; they are not assessed in annual performance reviews. And yet these are the skills that separate out the high performing managers from those who merely survive.

In many organisations, PQ skills have not emerged onto the radar screen of HR departments because the HR department has not been looking in the right direction. Elsewhere, the whole idea of political effectiveness is seen as slightly grubby and disreputable: it is seen as naked careerism and stabbing colleagues and bosses in the back.

PQ skills are no more about personal advancement than IQ or EQ: they are about becoming more effective in the organisation. As organisations downsize, re-engineer, become more matrixed, complicated and hollowed out, so the importance of PQ skills rises. In a traditional command and control organisation it is relatively simple to know where the power lies and what levers to pull to make things happen: ask the boss. In a complex matrix, managers cannot rely on their bosses to call the shots. Managers have to build their own sources of power. These sources of power are the networks of influence and alliances of mutual interest which actually make things happen. Informal power is now an essential part of a manager's toolkit.

Obviously, PQ has not suddenly emerged out of nowhere. Political skills have always been important, just as IQ and EQ have always been important. Machiavelli's *The Prince*, published in 1532, is testimony to the long lasting importance of political skills. But until recently, political skills have remained in the political arena: they were important for politicians and other elected officials. Political skills were not seen as being important in the workplace. Calling a manager "political" is still an insult rather than a compliment to a manager. Political skills are ancient skills which are new to the workplace.

Developing IQ, EQ and PQ: a sea change in management development

Many organisations implicitly assume that you either have IQ, EQ and PQ or you do not. Organisations will happily test for IQ, but they will not suggest that they can raise your IQ. If you have it, you get in. If you don't, goodbye. This makes the idea of IQ, EQ and PQ very dangerous: it assumes that good managers are born not bred. England, and most of the world, had a 1000-year experiment in which leaders were born, not bred: they called it the aristocracy and royalty. It meant that we enjoyed having murderers, thieves, lunatics and incompetents (along with the odd hero or genius) ruling for 1000 years. Elected officials may not be much better, but going back to a world where managers and leaders are born not bred is not an attractive proposition, unless you are an aristocrat.

The good news for managers is that IQ, EQ and PQ are not innate characteristics which we either have or lack. They are a series of discrete skills which we can all learn. They are skills like playing a sport or a musical instrument: we may never become an international star, but with training and practice we can become more competent.

Business IQ is different from academic IQ. University professors tend not to make great business leaders: most of them find it difficult running their own departments. Business IQ skills involve things such as:

- making decisions
- solving problems
- managing budgets

- thinking strategically
- organising projects
- preparing spreadsheets and presentations
- reviewing documents
- analysing data

In some firms, this is called "business judgement". That implies you either have it or you don't. That is a fatalistic view which helps neither the business nor the manager. In practice, these skills can be learned. Technical training helps, but it is not the full answer. For instance, technical training helps with building spreadsheets. But understanding spreadsheets from a management perspective is little to do with either IT skills or numeracy. Understanding spreadsheets means testing assumptions, knowing the business and knowing the person who is presenting the spreadsheet: some people are more credible than others.

At the heart of most management IQ is experience, not academic brilliance. This sounds like an excuse for keeping young people in junior positions. It is not. In practice, experience can be acquired at warp speed. The path to the top can be accelerated by learning from the accumulated experience of other people in the same company or in similar positions. This has nothing to do with teaching business school orthodoxy or learning theory: it is about learning what works in practice in your context.

Decisiveness is often seen as an innate quality of good managers: some people are decisive, some are indecisive and some think they are decisive but keep on changing their minds. Even something like decisiveness can be learned from experience: once you have seen a movie five times you know what comes next. Once you have seen five crises, or five different people underperforming or five political logjams with the same department, you recognise the pattern. Decisiveness is less a matter of innate character: it is simply pattern recognition. Learning decisiveness is then a matter of learning the patterns. Crisis management companies are good at crisis management not because of the natural management talent, but because they have learned from experience and recognise the patterns.

There are brilliant people with high IQs who make good managers; there are also people with modest IQs who do very well. Fortunately, firms and managers do not have to assume that management IQ is a birth right: we can build individual and institutional IQ by codifying and sharing experience and practice of what works.

EQ follows the same pattern as IQ. There are plenty of tests available to tell you what your EQ is. But we can build our management EQ once we think of EQ as a series of discrete and learnable skills. For managers EQ is not about being liked, it is about being effective. Managers must know how to get the most out of other people sustainably. That means managers need a toolkit of core EQ skills such as:

- motivating people (long term)
- influencing and persuading skills
- coaching
- delegating
- managing upwards
- overcoming resistance
- adapting to different styles and situations
- managing yourself: time, emotion, style

As with IQ, most of these EQ skills are learned through experience and pattern recognition. There are plenty of books and courses which claim to give the perfect solution to motivating, influencing or coaching. They offer some help by giving managers a framework to think about their own experience, and they give some ideas on how to improve. Most managers find that reality is more difficult and more complicated than the theory in the book or the course. Even the best framework has to be adapted to each manager's style and situation. In other words, experience and pattern recognition trump theory.

The importance of pattern recognition and experience means that management development has to change. There will still be a place for books, courses and theory: they are all based, to some extent, on accumulated experience of thousands of managers. But managers want to learn about what works in their context. The experience of people in other industries is interesting, but less relevant: teachers, army officers, bankers, chemists and civil servants may gain some insight from talking to each other. But when they want to know what really works, they rightly turn to peers who are in the same industry and same sort of context as each other. Peers understand the challenges each other faces.

Management development has to move away from the simple world of buying in training vendors. Even if they customise their offering, they are still imposing their world view on your reality. More effective development enables peers to learn from each other in a structured way. This is already starting to happen: in the education world "action learning sets" are a fancy way of describing how teachers can learn from each other. Peer group learning has contextual relevance and credibility which no outside vendor can bring. The role of the vendor is less about imparting their grand theory, and more about structuring and accelerating the process of peer to peer learning.

PQ: welcome to the revolution

PQ is at the heart of the revolution as managers experience it. Managing politics well is the key to succeeding and leading in the new world disorder. Managers can no longer rely on formal authority to make things happen. They must know how to acquire informal power and how to use it. It is another hurdle for managers to jump. Given that it is a new concept, it is worth exploring in a little more detail what it is and what it is not.

PQ is not about the dark arts of accelerating personal ambitions and stabbing peers in the back. That form of PQ has existed as long as humans have had communities. PQ is the art of making things happen in the organisation, especially where managers find that their responsibilities exceed their authority. PQ is about gaining the informal power required to achieve the formal requirements of the job. It is at the heart of management as most managers now experience it.

Outlined above are some of the core skills which make up PQ. At risk of repetition, here they are again:

- Building networks of trust and influence
- Creating alliances to make things happen
- Dealing with conflict
- Shaping the organisation's agenda to meet your needs
- Dealing with organisational conflict and resistance

- Managing ambiguity and uncertainty
- Finding the right assignments and projects to work on
- Discovering the real rules of survival and success in your firm

Understanding effective PQ is an emerging art. However, as with IQ and EQ there are consistent patterns of behaviour which mark out effective versus less effective PQ managers. These have been covered in *How to Lead* and, more completely, in *Power at Work*. A sample of four of these behaviours is set out below:

1. *Build a network.* Strong PQ managers build a network of informal influence and power. The network is not based on friendship. It is based on mutual interest and mutual respect. Power networks enjoy network economics: the stronger the network, the more attractive it becomes for other people to engage with it. Strong networks become stronger, while weak networks remain weak. This is visible in most organisations: power players attract power while people who are out of the loop find it very hard to break in. This is important for career management. When a very effective manager is head hunted to a new organisation, disaster often ensues. The effective manager was probably very effective because of the power network carefully cultivated over years with the last employer. In the new organisation, the power player has no power network and cannot make things happen. The power player suddenly becomes ineffective and eventually leaves, citing culture clashes and other reasons. The underlying reason is often about power and effectiveness.
2. *Build trust.* Building a network is easy to say, but hard to do. Networks are built up one node at a time. This requires

building trust with a range of people across the organisation: they will not have the same priorities, perspectives or personality as you. Trust in a business context reflects three factors:

(a) Find shared values, goals and priorities. This is partly about aligning business agendas: marketing and finance may have different priorities but both share the need to maximise the firm's profitability. Somewhere, common ground can be found. Good political operators will not just find the common rational ground (business priorities). They will also find common emotional ground: it might be shared interests beyond work or common attitudes about how things should work within work. Talking the same language starts to build trust.

(b) Demonstrate credibility. We may like people who share our values and priorities, but we will not trust them unless they can deliver on their promises. Credibility comes even from the smallest things, such as following up a meeting by sending out minutes or a thank you note fast. And if we fail to deliver on the large commitments, we are sunk. This requires more than politician's honesty: politicians assume they are honest until they are proven to be liars in a court of law. It is a recipe for dissembling and the abuse of language to say one thing while hiding something else. Business honesty has a higher hurdle. It requires setting and meeting expectations clearly: if expectations are not met, then you cannot use politician's words to escape the damage. Far from PQ being Machiavellian and deceitful, strong PQ rewards honesty and integrity.

(c) Manage risk. Most people are risk averse. The greater the risk, the more trust is required. I may trust a stranger to give me directions in the street: I will not trust a stranger with my life savings. For managers, this means that trust has to grow incrementally. When we show we can be trusted on small things, we earn the right to be trusted on larger things. If we have a big and risky proposal to promote, we need to break it down into bite sized chunks: create a pilot; do a proof of concept; phase the proposal so that each phase is lower risk.

3. *Take control.* John Major, when he was Prime Minister, was accused of being in office, but not in power. Power is not just about position: it is about how you use that position. You have to take control. With power, you use it or lose it. Strong PQ managers have two simple ways of taking control:

   (a) tell a story: if you are sophisticated, we can call this creating a vision. Tell a story which shows where your department is, where it is going and how it will get there. In other words, have a plan. And keep it simple: only the simplest plans will be remembered, let alone acted on. Simple means a story like "this year we are cutting costs" or "we will be first to market with the new widget" or "this year is all about quality and zero defects". A story lets you set priorities and focus effort; it tells you what you will not do so that you can focus on what is important. Creating simplicity out of complexity can be difficult and often takes courage, because it means making choices.

   (b) strike early: if you want to set the agenda, be first to suggest it. Anchor the discussion around your expectations. If you want to negotiate a good budget for next year, set expectations early and anchor the discussion. In any organisation, there are moments of uncertainty and doubt when no-one knows what to do: strong PQ managers will fill that void of uncertainty with a promise to take action. Striking early enables managers to take control and set the agenda on their terms, rather than allowing themselves to be dictated to by events.

4. *Pick your battles.* Organisations are full of conflict. The scope for conflict is increasing as organisations delayer and move from functional to matrix structures: managers now have to deal with a wider range of constituencies with more conflicting priorities. It pays to know which battles to fight. Sun Tsu, writing *The Art of War* over 2500 years ago outlined three rules of battle which apply today as much as ever:

- Only fight when there is a prize worth fighting for.
- Only fight when you know you will win.
- Only fight when you have no other way of achieving your goal.

Most corporate battles fail at least one, and sometimes all three, of these rules. High PQ managers know when to fight, partly because they are very focused on outcomes. If they know what is important and what they need to achieve, they know which battles they must fight.

Clearly, there is far more to the art of high PQ. Some of the other PQ skills include:

- how to claim credit (by appearing to give it away);
- how to have a claim to fame and to stake that claim;
- how to focus on outcomes and drive to results;
- how to find the sources of power in an organisation;

- how to look and act the part;
- how to find the right assignments and projects.

These skills reflect the daily reality and challenges of many managers. They help to differentiate successful from less successful managers. Although managers know these skills are important, none of them are tracked in appraisal systems, no training is provided and management theory virtually ignores these skills in favour of more traditional IQ and EQ type skills.

The prejudice against PQ skills is unhealthy for managers and for firms. Developing PQ develops the capacity of managers to make things happen in complex organisations. These are the practical skills that enable managers to be the glue which holds the organisation together. Managers who lead in the new world disorder will be managers with high PQ. Having a strong business IQ and EQ is no longer enough.

Conclusions

The job of the manager is changing out of all recognition. Managers are still the glue that holds the organisation together. But it is no longer about connecting the top and bottom of the organisation. It is about connecting together a network of power and influence to make things happen through other people. This requires a changed set of skills. No longer does the manager have to get ideas out of his head and into the hands of the unthinking workers. The job is not just command and control. The job is about orchestrating the skills of the network, helping the organisation discover and deliver the best solution. The job has changed from instructing to enabling. That makes the manager's job harder but more rewarding. In addition to traditional IQ skills, managers have to acquire EQ and PQ skills. Although these are new skills, they are all skills that can be learned. Increasingly, managers can control their own destiny.

Chapter Eleven

Leaders: No More Heroes

Most revolutions have leaders, who are heroes to some and villains to others. We may like or loathe Lenin, Mao Tse Tung and Napoleon, but we cannot doubt that they changed the world. These bloodthirsty revolutionaries tended to wreak economic havoc with their countries. This is an ignoble tradition which many business and banking leaders have copied by wreaking economic havoc arising from the credit crunch.

But the business revolution is not about leaders. It is about the way management works. It is about leadership, not leaders. We will not see any business leader waving a revolutionary flag and announcing a new world order. Instead, we are seeing the very nature of leadership change. The old orthodoxy is giving way to a new type of leadership.

The new world disorder is challenging established beliefs about leadership. In this chapter we will explore three challenges to leadership, and suggest some solutions to each challenge:

1. The cult of the leader as a hero is alive and well – and it is counterproductive.
2. Anglo-Saxon ideas of leadership are reaching their sell-by date.
3. Leadership development, and the MBA in particular, is a broken model.

The cult of the leader

Everyone likes a hero. From Batman and Superman to Churchill and Mandela, fact and fiction focus on the heroes who save the world. The business world is no different. Business leaders are held up as heroes when they succeed. When their firms go bust, the heroes become villains. In boom or bust, the media focus on the people at the top of the firm. They get their photo in the *Financial Times* or a nice pen drawing in the *Wall Street Journal*. Stories about people and personalities sell newspapers. Stories about management systems do not.

In good times, the heroes are eulogised. Fred Goodwin was named Fred the Shred for his ability to cut costs and build profits at Royal Bank of Scotland. When the bank went bust as a result of the bank's failed policies, Fred the Shred became Fred the Dead. He became the pantomime villain who was maximising his payouts and pensions from a bank that he broke. Personalising the success and failure of RBS is entertaining but misleading. Fred was not acting alone. Nor was RBS the only financial institution to fail: in late 2008 the great names of banking either went bust, had to be bailed out, or got taken over: AIG, Lehman Brothers, Bear Sterns,

Merrill Lynch, Fannie Mae, RBS and HBOS were among the more prominent failures. Focusing on the leader as hero or villain does not help us understand the real causes of success or failure in most firms and industries. Systemic success and failure is about the system, not about an individual. This makes the very high pay of a few leaders hard to justify.

The cult of the hero leader is not just a media fancy. It is also celebrated within the firm. Newsletters and annual reports are like *Pravda* in the Soviet era: unreliable eulogies of praise to the great leader (and some of the heroic workers). The myth of the great leader is also embedded in the boardroom. Since 1965 the median pay of CEOs in the US has risen from 20 times average income to 200 times average income. Mean CEO pay has risen even further, to 275 times average income. A typical worker would have to work for six lifetimes to earn what a typical CEO earns in one year. Part of this explosion in CEO pay is technical. The remuneration committee looks at the benchmark for CEO pay and decides that their CEO must be above average (why hire the CEO otherwise?) and so they pay above average. The benchmark then rises and every other remuneration committee ups their CEO's salary. CEO salaries live on a one way escalator: there is an up escalator, but no down escalator. But the greater part of the explosion of CEO pay comes from a growing belief in the CEO as hero: the solution to all the firm's problems is to hire the great CEO who will magically change everything, provided we pay enough. The challenges of many firms are way beyond the capabilities of any hero. Even Hercules would have shied away from cleaning out GM and Ford.

Some reality exists behind the hype around great leaders. Entrepreneurs often fit the hero mould of leadership. Carnegie, JP Morgan and Morita (Sony) in previous generations; Branson,

Mittal and Murdoch in this generation all dazzle us. Their organisations would not exist without their vision and drive. Their wealth is beyond our wildest dreams. Future generations will continue to be dazzled by the next generation of great entrepreneurs who will build great wealth and great enterprises.

But the vast bulk of enterprises are legacy organisations, where the founders have long since moved on. These organisations do not depend on the genius of one individual. They depend on the system as a whole. Warren Buffet observed this obliquely when he wrote: "I only invest in companies which any fool can run, because some day some fool will run it." If a fool can run a successful company, then the cult of the highly paid hero leader seems to be a waste of money.

Collins and Porras in *Built to Last* showed in their study of long term successful companies that there is no need for a hero leader. The CEOs of many of the most successful companies are not household names. Nearly every household has a few P&G products: detergents, toiletries, paper products or cosmetics. Most people would be hard pressed to name any P&G leaders. Since P&G was formed in 1837 it has maintained a steady goal of doubling its real size every 10 years. That does not sound like much, but over 170 years that has enabled P&G to become an $83 billion turnover global giant. You do not need to take heroic actions to become a giant. Equally, most people could not name the current CEOs of Toyota or Honda while the CEOs of struggling Ford and GM get a much higher profile. Few have heard of the CEOs of the world's most successful professional service firms like Deloitte, PwC, Clifford Chance, Linklaters or Baker & McKenzie. Lasting success whispers, instant success or failure shouts. We need to listen more carefully to the whispers of success.

If we do not need our leaders to be heroes, then what should they be?

Based on interviews and surveys with over 2000 leaders in the public, private and voluntary sectors I have found what we expect of people who lead us. The top five qualities we expect of our leaders are reassuringly simple:

- Vision
- Ability to motivate others
- Decisiveness
- Ability to handle crises
- Honesty and integrity

We will examine what each of these mean in practice. But before we do so, note what is not there. There is nothing about charisma or inspiration. Inspiration maybe nice to have, but it is not necessary. This is just as well. None of the leaders I interviewed could be accused of being charismatic and inspirational, but all were highly effective in their own organisations. You cannot teach charisma or inspiration, and medical science has yet to devise the charisma implant. All the other qualities we expect of a leader can be learned to a greater or lesser degree of proficiency. In practice, firms do not need inspirational leaders. Firms need professional leaders.

Let's look at what we really need of our leaders.

Vision

Visions are dangerous. For every leader who leads you to the Promised Land, there are another dozen who lead you straight back into the desert. President Kennedy's vision of fighting communism led America to the moon, but also to Vietnam. For business leaders, visions do not have to be grand or heroic. You do not have to be like Martin Luther King saying "I have a dream ..." If you dream in the office, keep it to yourself. A vision is much simpler. It is a story in three parts:

- This is where we are
- This is where we are going
- This is how we will get there

To make it compelling and motivational, leaders add a fourth element: "this is your important role in helping us all get there." In other words, make the vision personal and relevant to each individual: raising EPS by 15% may be important but it does not mean much to the janitor.

Ability to motivate others

Leaders do poorly on this: only 46% of respondents rate their leader as being any good at motivating their team. Motivation is more than one minute managing people with some synthetic complement. Equally, leaders do not have the time or energy to become fully qualified psychologists. There has to be a middle way. We found one question which, if answered positively, causes the leader to be rated well on more or less everything else. That question was "My boss is interested in me and my career" (Agree/Disagree). Show you genuinely care for each individual: look after them and they will look after you. It may sound simple, but it is not. In the day to day grind of administrivia, politics and crises it is easy to forget to look after the team. And each person has different needs. But investing time in the team normally yields high returns.

Decisiveness

Decisiveness sounds like one of those mysterious qualities such as good judgement or charisma, which you either have or you do not have. Decisiveness is not innate: it can be learned. Decisive leaders typically have two advantages over more indecisive people:

- They have clear vision, clear values and clear priorities. This makes it far easier to decide between two courses of action which otherwise look equally attractive.
- They have seen the movie before. If you have seen the same pattern of events unfold before, it is easier to predict what will happen next. You do not have to wait 25 years to acquire such experience. You can learn from others' experience how to deal with even the most awkward situations, such as dealing with underperformance issues.

Ability to handle crises

Fear, uncertainty and doubt are the natural companions of most crises. Followers value leaders who can remove fear, uncertainty and doubt: good leaders create clarity and hope in even the darkest situations. They drive to action and focus on the future rather than analysing the past or blaming others. As with decisiveness, much of crisis management can be learned. Crisis management companies succeed not because of the innate brilliance of their managers, but because of the experience they have accumulated. It is the same with leaders: learning from personal experience and the experience of others improves a leader's ability to handle crises well.

Honesty and integrity

For business leaders, honesty and integrity is not about preaching morality and ethics. It is more important and more sustainable than that. Honesty and integrity is fundamentally about trust. Colleagues and customers do not want to work with someone they do not trust. Building trust involves showing that you have some common values and goals; showing that you can deliver on what you say and dealing promptly even with the more uncomfortable situations all leaders face. Honesty and integrity was highly divisive. Anyone who scored low on this, scored low on everything else.

The overwhelming message from this research is that we do not expect our leaders to be charismatic superheroes. We expect them to be professional. The skills of a professional and effective leader can be learned.

The Anglo-Saxon leader's sell-by date

The literature on leadership is dominated by an Anglo-Saxon view of the world. Three of the leading books on management and leadership over the last 30 years have been based more or less exclusively on an American view of the world. *In Search of Excellence*, *Built to Last* and *Good to Great* cover 88 companies. Of the 88, only one is not American: *Built to Last* included Sony, which is run by a Welshman who made good in America.

Thirty years ago, perhaps it was possible to believe that the American model of management and leadership was not just dominant: it was the only model of successful management. Since that time American supremacy has been challenged by the rise of Asia.

Asia has not just been a source of cheap labour, providing clothes and toys for WalMart. It has challenged entire industries such as Auto manufacturing and consumer electronics where America once dominated. In 2008 Toyota finally overtook GM as the world's largest auto manufacturer.

The credit crunch has generated much media hand wringing about the end of capitalism. Even Jack Welch, who ran GE ruthlessly for the benefit of shareholders, recanted, saying "On the face of it, shareholder value is the dumbest idea in the world." Despite the sensationalism, capitalism is not over. But it is time to recognise that there are other ways of leading and succeeding. The global economic battle is not just about different forms of capitalism and different sources of comparative advantage. It is also about different ways of leading.

As a simple test, I undertook a paired comparison of British and French styles of leadership, in partnership with Oxford University. On the face of it, they should not be much different. On a clear day, both countries can see each other across the Channel. The sixth largest French city, ranked by number of French citizens living there, is London: it was an early call on President Sarkozy's election trail in 2007. A summary of the headline results are below: Subsequent interviews revealed the depth of the differences between UK and French leadership styles:

- The French place much more emphasis on the "old school tie": going to ENA or one of the other Grandes Ecoles was a passport to career advancement and a network of influence. Over half of French Prime Ministers have graduated from ENA, which turns out just over 100 graduates a year. ENA makes Oxford or Harvard graduates look like a populist rabble by comparison.

Table 11.1 Top five expectations of a good leader in the UK and France

United Kingdom	France
Vision	Ability to handle crises
Ability to motivate others	Network strength
Decisiveness	Ability to motivate others
Ability to handle crises	Decisiveness
Honesty and integrity	Political skills

- Decision making is very different: French talk about British pragmatism and flexibility. This is a polite way of saying that the British flip flop and go with whatever works, whereas the French will work out the intellectually correct decision, and then stick to it.
- Communication and authority are viewed differently. French leaders expect to explain their decision clearly, once, and then everyone will follow their intellectual lead. The British will spend more time persuading and convincing. They will not rely purely on authority to convey the message: they will seek commitment to a decision, not just compliance. The French method works where you have command and control; the British method works better in more ambiguous situations.

By the end of the study it became clear why the British and the French have spent their mutual history being the best of enemies and the best of allies. They are very close and very different at the same time. The one thing that the French would agree on was that German leadership was a complete nightmare: no intellectual rigour, just a focus on practical detail leading to extraordinary inflexibility. Naturally, the Germans have a somewhat different view.

If there are this many differences when you take a train beneath the Channel, then the differences multiply as you go to different cultures. A highly prejudiced snapshot of some of these differences across cultures is captured in Table 11.2.

This compares British, French, Japanese and Traditional leadership styles. The Japanese assessment is based on three years of building a business in Japan. The view from traditional societies is based on seven years of original research with tribes from Mali to Mongolia and the Arctic to Australia via Papua New Guinea and beyond. Before we dismiss the traditional view too quickly, it is worth noting that traditional societies have survived for far longer in far harsher conditions than most Western organisations. Less than 20% of the original S&P 500 have survived the last 50 years. A tribe which only survives one generation is not a success, and they have to survive without bankers, consultants, lawyers, accountants, HR staff, IT Help Desks, computers, phones, electricity or running water. In tough times, we have something to learn from them.

Japan is different. It feels less like a different country and more like a different planet. If Japan is perplexing to us, then the West is often perplexing to Japan. One Japanese business leader finally screwed up the courage to ask me a question which had been nagging him for ages: "Owen-san, how do you shake hands?" I was staggered. The Japanese ritual of bowing seemed incomprehensible to me, while shaking hands is simple. Now try explaining hand shaking rules to a Japanese. When do you shake hands? Who makes the first move? How do you know the other person wants to shake hands? How long and how hard do you shake hands? What are you meant to say? Suddenly, bowing seemed simple by comparison because at least there are clear rules, and a *meishi* (business card)

Table 11.2 Leadership styles across the world

Factor	UK	Japan	Traditional societies	France
Decision processes	Pragmatic, well communicated	Consensual	Communal, open	Top down, well thought through
Hierarchy	Call boss by first name	Respect based language	Age and sex	Tu, vous, title depending on relationship
Networks	Based on profession	Based on keiretsu	Family based	Academic background
Education focus	Liberal arts	Maths, science, engineering	Informal, oral, generalists	Maths and science
Key industries	City, services, media.	Engineering, manufacturing	Subsistence	Engineering, luxury goods
Values	Ethics, spirit of the law	Honesty and trust, outside law	Respect for the community	Honesty, letter of the law
Delegation	Responsibility exceeds authority	Collective responsibility	Compartmentalisation	Responsibility requires authority
Feedback	Indirect, often positive	Avoided	No	Direct, often negative: teach
Body language	Hidden; appears devious	Formality, ritual	Open	Open and direct
Openness	Wimbledonisation of London	Closed	Binary	Closed: revolution not evolution
Law	Common law, flexible	Avoid using law	Tradition, personal	Roman law; highly prescriptive
Thinking	Pragmatic	Practical	Tradition	Theoretical, based on principles
Meetings	Make decisions	Confirm decisions	Social	Air views, defend position,

will tell everything about a person's status which in turn tells you who should bow first, deepest and longest. If such a trivial thing is so different, then the more important matters such as decision making, power and authority, motivation and all other leadership matters involve profound differences.

This is not the time or place to do an extensive anthropological review of cross-cultural leadership styles. It is enough to note that there are profound differences, that the differences matter and that we cannot assume that the Anglo-Saxon model of leadership is the only viable model of leadership. A couple of examples will suffice to make the point, even at the risk of painting caricatures. There are as many differences within a culture as there are across cultures. But, as ever, the caricatures point to differences which are relatively common.

Thinking and decision making

We have already noted the difference between the pragmatic/flexible British and the intellectual French. The Japanese differ again: they tend to be intensely practical, focused on detail. And they build consensus: meetings do not make decisions, they confirm in public agreements which have already been made in private. The result is slow decision making but rapid implementation. That is the opposite of many Anglo-Saxon firms which often have fast decision making and slow implementation. Traditional societies differ again, by going back to tradition and oral history to determine decisions. Precedent is a very powerful principle in non literate cultures.

Networks

We have already seen the power of French old school tie networks, contrasting with the power of professional and personal networks in the Anglo-Saxon world (and some business school networks). In Japan, networks are still based on *keiretsu*: these are associations of companies linked by cross-shareholdings and often arranged around one of the great Japanese trading companies (*sogo shosha*) such as Marubeni, Itochu, Mitsui and Mitsubishi Corporation. The revenues of each of these *sogo shosha* are greater than the GDP of Switzerland. In traditional societies, networks are based on family ties, which makes marriage a doubly significant event. The Chinese diaspora across South East Asia is also based on family networks; within mainland China *guanxi* (connections, especially to government) are essential.

Hierarchies
In the Anglo-Saxon world bosses are called by their Christian names. At least the veneer of equality and democracy is maintained in a very unequal and undemocratic relationship. France enjoys the complexity of *tu* and *vous*, while Japan goes further and has perhaps the world's only respect based language. Every time you open your mouth, you not only convey meaning, but you also confirm your status relative to the person you are talking to: grammar and words change depending on who has more status. Status is based on position in the firm, the prestige of the firm and whether you are a supplier or a customer. Women borrow their husband's status. Hierarchy in the tribal world is based on age and sex, with clear compartmentalisation of roles and elaborate rites of passage from one stage to the next.

By now it should be clear that there are fundamentally different views of leadership, management and organisation across the world. The dominant literature, based on an American world view, looks very limited and parochial. When America was the dominant and most successful world economy, such a narrow view could be justi-fied. Now that the rest of the world is not only catching up, but in some areas leaping ahead, we need to expand our horizons and recognise that there different models of leadership out there.

Ultimately, this is liberating for management. We do not have to follow some academic's theory of leadership. Nor do we have to ape the formulas being promoted by self-serving entrepreneurs and business leaders in their autobiographies. There is room out there to create our own leadership formula. Our leadership formulas reach far beyond the narrow confines of personality differences, described by MB/TI (Myers Briggs Type Indicators) and others.

The new orthodoxy which is emerging is that leadership is con-textual. What works in one context may not work in another context. For example, risk is the lifeblood of a trader on Wall Street, but it is like Kryptonite to a civil servant in Washington. The trader will embrace risk, the civil servant will avoid it. Both the trader and the civil servant take the correct approach, in their respective contexts. Arguably, traders take too much risk and civil servants take too little: that is a matter of policy and debate. What cannot be doubted are the different approaches taken in different contexts.

The contextual approach to leadership is so obvious that it has been completely missed by the gurus who all claim to have dis-covered the unique formula for universal leadership success. As George Orwell noted: "to see what is in front of your nose requires constant struggle". It is a struggle which has been beyond the capa-bility of the gurus with their quack formulas for success.

If leadership is contextual, that raises some interesting challenges about how we can learn to lead. It implies that we cannot apply a formula, read a book or listen to a speech and suddenly be transformed into a leader by discovering some secret formula for leadership. How we learn to lead is explored in the next section.

Leadership development, and the MBA in particular, is a broken model

Think, for a moment, about how you have learned to lead. This is a question I have now asked thousands of executives, and it is one question to which I receive consistent answers. To make your choice simpler, pick two out of the following six methods as your main ways of acquiring your method of leadership:

- Books
- Courses
- Bosses (good or bad lessons)
- Role Models (inside or outside work)
- Peers
- Experience

Virtually no-one chooses books or courses. This could be bad news for someone who writes books and offers courses. It also puts in question the value of the whole leadership development industry, if no-one finds they learn from the courses offered. But it is a natural response. You cannot start reading a book at page 1 and finish at page 276 as a leader, even if the book is mine: *How to Lead*.

In practice, people learn to lead from their own experience and from the experience of others. They see someone do something smart, and they decide to copy it themselves. If it works, they add it to their repertoire of skills. They see someone mess up and quietly make a note to avoid making the same mistake. Everyone creates their own leadership method which is as unique as their own DNA, but it has been based on begging, borrowing and stealing little bits of leadership DNA from lots of other people.

Learning from experience makes the path to leadership a random walk. This is wasteful and time consuming. Get the right experiences, and you find the high road to success. Get unlucky with your experiences, assignments and bosses and you will find yourself wandering in a jungle of underachievement. This is where the books and courses can come in useful. The better books and courses will help you put some structure on your random walk of experience; they will help you accelerate your process of learning from experience and will help you develop your own unique formula for success.

The worst books and courses attempt to give you a universal formula to follow: at its nadir this means sitting in a group trying to guess what the facilitator is meant to write on the flip chart so that it conforms to the franchised theory he has paid for. The alternative, slightly more entertaining, version comes in the form of motivational speakers: they will want us to believe that they have cracked the leadership code because they were the first people to go up Everest, on a pogo stick backwards and naked. The entertainment value is normally inversely related to the practical value of such speeches. At this point, the Bible offers us a timely reminder of how to treat such people: "Beware false prophets ... many false prophets shall rise and shall deceive many" (Matthew 7:15 and 24:11.)

Given the nature of most books and courses it is not surprising to find that training budgets are among the first to be cut in tough times. And much of the training is not missed. The CIPD (Chartered

Institute for Personnel Development) ran a study to find out why people resisted training. The top five reasons were:

* They are too busy at work
* Family or personal commitments
* They are insufficiently motivated
* Resistance from line managers
* Insufficient culture of learning at work

These reasons need a little translation, provided below:

* They are too busy at work (= not a priority for me)
* Family or personal commitments (= not a priority for me)
* They are insufficiently motivated (= not a priority for me)
* Resistance from line managers (= not a priority for my boss)
* Insufficient culture of learning at work. (= not a priority for anyone)

The resistance to training increases with seniority. A new executive might be keen to pick up some new skills. In particular, there is an appetite for technical skills. There is no great shame in admitting you need to learn more about finance. But going on a course on motivation implies that you do not know how to handle people well. It is a weakness that we do not readily admit to. This fear of admitting weakness increases with seniority. A senior executive with 20 years of relative success to look back on will not take kindly to some trainer with a theory coming along to challenge that success formula. Managers stick with what works in practice, not what works in theory.

The gulf between theory and practice is most evident in the MBA course. We have already noted that leaders claim to learn mainly from bosses, role models, peers and experience and that books and courses are more or less irrelevant to them. An MBA is based on books and courses.

An MBA is not entirely without merit. An MBA does two things for a student. First and foremost it is an elaborate executive placement agency which helps students either redirect or accelerate their careers. Business schools provide good quality control for recruiters. Career switching and acceleration is a service worth paying for. Second, business schools codify and transmit a body of knowledge from one generation to the next: this has always been a major purpose of most academic institutions. Knowledge which can be codified is explicit knowledge: things like finance, accounting and to some extent marketing, strategy and organisation design. These are technical skills which are well worth acquiring. But the skills which leaders really need to acquire now are much harder to codify or transmit.

Motivating people, managing politics, creating networks of influence and trust, managing your boss, dealing with conflict and crises, getting the right assignments and actually making things happen are difficult skills to codify or teach. Part of the problem is that each person has a different way of doing these things, and the ideal way of doing them depends on your context: chemicals companies, voluntary organisations, investment banks, the civil service and different nationalities all have different rules of survival and success. The MBA is caught in a time warp, where management is fundamentally a rational and intellectual discipline. Anyone who has been in an organisation and has been capable of fogging a mirror will know that organisations are not purely rational: they are deeply political places full of humans with hopes and fears. If you cannot manage the politics and the emotion, you cannot manage the organisation. These really important skills, these tacit skills, are beyond the effective reach of business schools. This is unfortunate because Harvard Business School, on its website, claims it is "focused on one purpose – developing leaders". The tacit skills of leadership are the one thing it cannot teach. The MBA is a well named degree: it is a masters in business *administration*. It can teach administrative and technical skills. It does not produce great leaders, despite the hype of Harvard.

Henry Mintzberg and Joseph Lampel tracked 19 "superstars" to have graduated from HBS who later became CEOs. Here is what Mintzberg found: "Ten were outright failures (the company went bankrupt, the CEO was fired, a major merger backfired etc.); another four had questionable records at best. Five out of the 19 seemed to do fine. These figures, limited as they were, sounded pretty damning."

The credit crunch has been fuelled by MBAs who rose to the tops of financial institutions where they made huge amounts of money while their firms went bankrupt. Neither Harvard nor the MBA can be blamed entirely for this, but they are part of the problem rather than part of the solution. The case method assumes that one evening you know nothing about MegaBucks: you read a case overnight and next day you can determine MegaBucks' future. The MBA breeds generations of ambitious individuals who have some technical competence but no leadership capability. It is little surprise that most of them go into the safe professional worlds of consulting or banking: you do not need great leadership capability to trade a bond or prepare a PowerPoint presentation.

Meanwhile, entrepreneurs who need real leadership talent are notable for being largely MBA free zones: Gates, Buffet, Jobs, Branson, Mittal, Abramovich have all escaped the curse of the MBA.

Conclusions

Like all other success in business, leadership is contextual. Different patterns of survival and success depend on your personal style, and on which industry and which country you work in. The search for orthodoxy is a waste of time: there is no universal formula for success. In particular, the conventional wisdom that American leadership is a universal model for success is over: the rise of Asia shows that there are other models and those models can be as successful as the American model. This makes the bulk of the leadership industry, and many books and courses, redundant. The suspicion with which practising managers approach leadership courses and books is well founded. There are some good offerings out there: many more are rubbish. The MBA is not about leadership: it is about career management and giving people a few technical management skills.

All of this is good news for aspiring leaders. We do not need to subscribe to the latest theory and try to be someone else. We need to create our own formula for success, based on our own experience and on observing the success and failure of peers, bosses and role models. Books and courses only help by offering some frameworks and giving some structure to the random walk of experience.

Our freedom to learn is not just an opportunity: it is a necessity. If we are to compete with the rest of the world we need to learn from them if we are not to be beaten by them. We need to shed our insularity. Real leadership is not about following the received wisdom and subscribing to the current orthodoxy. That is no more than acting as a steward of a legacy. Real leadership is about taking people where they would not have gone by themselves. That requires changing and innovating to meet a constantly changing world. We have the freedom to be different, but we also have the responsibility to be different if we are to make an impact as leaders.

Conclusion

Modern management has helped humanity achieve extraordinary prosperity and progress. Management was built on the ideals of the Enlightenment which drove the Industrial Revolution: enquiry, measurement, improvement and science. This led to the search for formulas to help managers and firms improve strategy, leadership, financial management, quality and productivity. These formulas were devastatingly effective. They blew away old practices based on rule of thumb and experience.

But now modern management is reaching its end game. The simplistic formulas are no longer building blocks for success, but building blocks for failure. Gaining competitive advantage is difficult when everyone is applying the same rules of strategy, leadership, finance and organisation with people of broadly similar calibre. The result is what we see in many industries: competitive stalemate where management have to run faster every year simply to stay still relative to the competition. It is a brutal way to survive.

The magic success formulas have lost their magic. The great companies we are meant to copy have a disturbing habit of falling by the wayside just as much as companies which are less exposed to the hype of gurus and academics. Established incumbents are challenged by upstarts with no resources but a good idea and plenty of ambition. Firms which are successful find it difficult to adapt and change to upstarts who appear to be playing to a different set of rules, a different formula. Suddenly a formula for success becomes a prison from which established firms cannot escape.

The old success formulas are failing because the world is changing: the new world needs new approaches. The changes are not small: they are vast. Power is shifting from producers to consumers, from West to East and from shareholders to managers. Both managers and firms are specialising more and more. Value chains are fragmenting and globalising at the same time. New competitors appear out of nowhere. Technology is enabling these changes, but we still have to learn how to control the technology before it controls us.

The tyranny of conformity is being replaced by the tyranny of freedom. The comforting formulas of the past no longer work; the dependence on a single employer for a job for life has gone. Freedom comes with responsibility, stress and ambiguity. We are not just free to change the rules: we have to work out what the rules of survival and success are for ourselves and our firms.

Firms face a choice about how to cope with the new world. Most established firms will continue to run ever faster on the treadmill of incremental improvement: improving quality, introducing new products, rationalising and reorganising both production and management, defending their existing markets. The future will be built by firms which dare to be different, introducing new business models and new ideas. Many will fail, but the successful ones will be the giants of tomorrow.

Managers must also learn new ways of succeeding. Managers are no longer ciphers between the top and bottom of the organisation.

Command and control has given way to coordination and commitment: coordinating the different functions of the firm and building commitment from people over whom they have no control. To make things happen, managers need not just the intellectual and interpersonal skills of the past. They also need the political skills to align the organisation behind their agenda. This is a more demanding but potentially more satisfying world than ever before.

Technology helps and hinders managers. It helps by improving personal productivity. It hinders by raising expectations and giving managers no escape from work. We may leave work, but work never seems to leave us.

No-one can tell what the future holds. This book does not pretend to predict. It simply maps the revolution unfolding around us. With this map, we can all make our choices about the journey we want to travel. It is a journey with great risk and great opportunity. Whatever choices you make, and whatever your journey is, enjoy it.

Index

Index compiled by Indexing Specialists (UK) Ltd